Eila!
Wishing you all the best with your
future still filled with Faith, Hope
and Love,   Janis

ajambel@shaw.ca

Print edition ISBN: 978-0-9920608-7-9

Electronic edition ISBN: 978-0-9920608-8-6

Published by Bible School Dropout Publications
Sault Ste. Marie, ON. CA.
bibleschooldropout@gmail.com

Cover Photo: Arno Ambel as Zorba in the 1993 Sault Opera production of *Zorba. Sault Opera: Zorba 1993 2004.10 Scrapbook 55 Courtesy of Sault Ste. Marie Public Library (ssmpl.ca).*

Mr. Opera!

Arno's Story

By: Janis Ambel

ACKNOWLEDGEMENTS

As an inexperienced writer I found the help of my dear 97 year old friend, Joan Summers (Grandma Joey), invaluable. I am grateful for her assistance in this venture.

Stephen Olar, thank you for using your exceptional skills to edit my book. Words cannot express how much I appreciate all the hard work and many hours you have spent to bring this project to completion.

Thank you so much Steve.

Janis

Arno's Story

FORWORD

In his memoirs, Harry S. Truman said much is lost when so few tell their own stories. It helps others to know what was in their minds and what impelled them to do what they did.

No one can know all the processes and stages of another's thinking in making important decisions. Others never know all the reasons why a person does certain things and why they come to certain conclusions. No one else can tell the events as that person saw them (Truman, 1956).

Although Arno Ambel did not tell his story, I believe it is an important one to share. His life had a tremendous impact on so many.

Arno achieved a great deal during his life. He changed the musical landscape of Sault Ste. Marie, Ontario Canada. He brought opera to a hockey-mad, steel town and succeeded. When we attend concerts or theatre productions now, there is an excellence in the quality of the work Arno helped to develop. He was well known for wanting to get it just right. He paved the way for many to be able to contribute their skills as well to our community.

He used the gift of music God gave him to enrich the lives of those around him. In spite of all his success he was still seeking for the deeper meaning of life.

His war experiences left him with unanswered questions and emotional unease. The dignity of each individual, the importance of freedom and each person's right to it was always there in the back of his mind. Every person has value and a purpose and no one else can fulfill that purpose.

Arno's country of birth, Estonia, has a history of foreign domination. With its coasts bordering waterways that were arms of the North Atlantic Ocean, countries saw the value of this land. In that day they knew that mastery of the ocean routes and free approach and entry to their ports was crucial to their military and economic success, or even keeping themselves alive.

Estonia's suffering under the control of these countries was unimaginable. None was worse than after World War II under Communist Russia.

Although Arno gained his freedom by coming to Canada, his parents were still trapped by Russian tyranny. His personal torment over this situation and the need for human dignity and personal freedom made him a very angry man. He had witnessed the degradation of the human heart caused by German and Russian oppression. For 19 years he was separated from his parents. Much of that time he did not know if they were alive. I think much of his drive and creativity served to help him deal with his inner pain.

Arno credited his survival during that time to God. Even though he continued to fight his internal demons for years, this same God eventually brought him inner peace.

My name is Janis Ambel. I met Arno later in life. His wife had passed away and so had my husband. A mutual friend introduced us. She and her husband invited the two of us to dine at a restaurant—and a courtship ensued. The characteristics Arno presented in his persistent pursuit for success in the field of music were the same qualities he used in pursuing me. He was a gentleman, but he was also tireless in his quest—he won my heart.

Janis Ambel
April 2014

Arno's Story

Chapter One

Where it all Began

In late autumn, 1926, in Tallinn, Estonia, Rudolf Friedrich and Liisu-Lisbeth Ambel eagerly anticipated the arrival of their second child. On November eighth they welcomed Arno Edgar into the world.

Arno's Father, Friedrich, was the manager of a prosperous hardware business owned by Mr. Edmund Hüppler. Friedrich was a tall, distinguished gentleman. A dapper man, he was seldom seen without a suit.

Arno's mother was an assistant to Mr. Hüppler's wife, Erika. She was also well known for the attractive garments she made. She had long brown hair, was an attractive, charming, and very personable lady.

The Hüpplers owned a large city block in which both families lived. They were very good friends. The Ambels were financially comfortable, which meant Arno was able to enjoy all the amenities that living in this block afforded them.

Tallinn played an important role in shaping Arno's perspective on life. That was where his roots were. His background, the history of the area, and the strength and depth of Estonian culture had a role in making him the man he became. Tallinn was dear to the hearts of those who called it home. It had a charm all its own.

The panoramic view of Tallinn from the Lasnamäe hill is picturesque. Below is the valley of Kadrioru. Farther down to the right, the Gulf of Finland glittered and beckoned through a filmy haze. Tallinn is a dynamic living city; slender spires of the cathedrals pierced the serene sky. Ancient towers juxtaposed against bright, modern buildings, lawns and hills, were reflected in the blue waters of the gulf (Viirlaid, p. 88).

Tallinn, with a current population of over 420,000, is the oldest capital city in Northern Europe. From the 13th century to the early 20th it was known as Ravel. The name of the city was changed when Estonia won its independence from Germany in 1918 (Tallinn, N.D.).

Archaeologists think the area was inhabited by ancestors of the present Estonians as far back as 2,500 years ago. Tallinn is considered one of the richest cities for its historical heritage. Twenty-seven mediaeval defense towers have been preserved. It is appropriately called a city of towers (German, pp. 7,11). Arno told me how he often walked along the top of these walls around the towers as a young boy. They held a fascination for him. There was something about being in such a stimulating place; the allure, the wonder of its history, drew him there time after time.

Arno had a fun loving nature and was always, always on the move. His older brother, Henry, kept him on his toes as brothers will do. He did not want to make it too easy for Arno. It would have been interesting to look on and see all the antics that went on.

They had a nanny, Minnie, whom Arno fondly remembered. She was an exceptional lady. A kind, caring lady, she poured her love on the boys and spoiled them. For many years Minnie spent June, July, and August with them in a summer home at the seaside town of Pirita.

The town is located approximately seven kilometers from Tallinn's center. It is one of the favorite places in Tallinn with its bathing beaches, coastline, pine-forested parks and picturesque Pirita River valley. Arno loved it there, beside the water, where he spent many summers during his youth. He particularly enjoyed swimming and became a proficient swimmer.

This set the brothers up later to be able to play water polo, at which they excelled. Arno was proud to be the goalie of his team. It is the most important position in the pool and the most exciting place to be in water polo, or any game for that matter.

You had to be tough to play water polo. A goalie is like a second coach in the water, the leader, and a director telling the players what to do and where to go. It is a game which requires an incredible amount of strategy and risk-taking. I don't doubt, the discipline he developed by playing water polo was a factor in the successes he achieved in other areas.

Tallinn's seaport was always brimming with activity. Arno and Henry enjoyed other sporting events and the yacht races which were part of the city's seaport life. He reveled in being alive in this setting. With his sense of humor and his energetic personality, there wouldn't have been a dull moment! He had quite the childhood! His life was care free and he enjoyed his youth with so many interesting things to do and places to go. He had many opportunities to learn skills and to live life to the fullest.

Tallinn was the cultural center of Estonia; the home of the Estonian Academy of Sciences, four higher-educational institutions, five professional theatres and 19 museums (German, p. 7). The people of Tallinn were passionate about cultural entertainment and knew how to spend their leisure hours. The theatres offered opera and ballet; places of fine musical traditions (German, p. 100).

Arno had the rare opportunity to learn opera as a young child. The Ambels lived next door to Armanda degli Abbati, an Italian mezzo-soprano, who starred in lead roles at La Scala, San Carlo, Torino, Covent Gardens and Paris. She also sang roles at St. Petersburg and later in Odessa.

In 1926 she was invited by the Estonian government to teach voice (Armanda degli Abbati-Campodonico, N.D.). Because her Master Classes were so successful, she also served as Vocal Coach for the Estonian Opera where she trained many of the leads. She worked with the Theatre of the Soviet Baltic Fleet as well. Imagine Arno being exposed to that kind of music all of the time!

When he was five Arno would listen to La Signorina degli Abbati's students singing next door. He told me laughingly about this period in his life, "If the student sang a wrong note, I would sing the right one."

His Mother would scold him severely for doing this but Signorina degli Abbati was amused. She took a special interest in him.

Signorina degli Abbati started training Arno when he turned seven. He studied voice with her for six years. He often said, "She took me under her wing and tried to make an opera singer out of me." From her he learned classic opera could be just as entertaining and amusing as any modern music. He enjoyed these performances and relished being involved in the arts.

She wrote a piece of music especially for him called "Väike Arno" (Little Arno). She gave him another piece of music, one which she had beautifully written by hand. On it she wrote, "To my beloved Arno." These original pieces of music can be seen at the Estonian Museum in Toronto.

He was inspired to write two original pieces of music at the age of 16. These are also in the same museum. His compositions, even then, were extraordinary; marked by depth and feeling. His hand-written music was impeccably done. He developed a passion for music which stayed with him all his life.

Friedrich, Arno's father was also known for his excellent voice. He sang in a choir which held concerts in and around the area, which were popular with concert goers. This was not the only gift Arno inherited from his Father.

Art was an important part of their family life as well. During his youth Fredrich studied painting from a very famous painter. Friedrich Ambel's paintings are skillfully and beautifully done. Arno was also skilled at painting and drawing.

Arno told me an interesting story about his father and a beautiful silver cigarette case. One day in the 1920's, his father had been gambling with Dr. Hirsch, who had been court physician for the late Russian Czar Nicholas II.

The Czar had a beautiful summer home in the area. Arno's father won the game and received the silver cigarette case as his prize. Czar Nicholas II had given Dr. Hirsch the case as a gift.

The front cover, etched in silver, has a dedication written: Yolka (Russian for Christmas) and Livadia (the name of the Czar's residence on the

Crimean peninsula) 1900. On the back of the case was inscribed the autographs of the Czar and his wife Alexandra.

Liisu-Lisbeth could neither paint nor carry a tune, but she appreciated art. She knew the libretti of the operas by heart. When his parents were finally able to come to Canada, she charmed the customs officials into allowing her to bring in her sterling silver flatware through customs—which was clearly prohibited by regulations.

From what Arno told me I think she was an amazing woman who was very perceptive to the events around her. She used this instinct for the survival of her family during the German and Russian occupations. Somehow she was able to discern the dangers involved and how to avoid the worst of them. I think Arno's survival instincts were inherited from his mother.

Arno's world was quickly changing to a darker place. In June, 1941, his beloved teacher, Signorina degli Abbati, was given the heart wrenching news that she would be deported to Siberia. Russia and Italy were at war and Armanda was an Italian citizen.

What a shame this great and talented woman should be valued so little and forced to suffer just because of her nationality. It was a disastrous ending to her life. She was taken to Harku prison in Estonia (Armanda degli Abbati-Campodonico, N.D.). The family believed she died in Siberia the next year. More than half of the people who were deported never returned. Most died of starvation.

Signorina degli Abbati's deportation occurred during a general deportation of approximately 11,000 Estonians on June 14th. Men, women and children were forcibly removed from their homes and families. On June 21, 1941, Germany invaded Estonia (Soviet Deportations from Estonia, N.D.).

Arno's parents were part of the highest level of Estonian Society. From an early age Arno was used to being treated with respect. Through this tragedy his eyes began to open to the forces of evil in others which can inflict so much pain, cruelty and death in the world.

The family learned of the tragic details of his brother's death. Henry was tortured and killed by the Russian secret police for defending his fiancée. The darkness had penetrated his family. They reeled from the shock.

Despite what was happening in Estonia and the rest of Europe, Arno was still able to continue his vocal studies with Eedo Karrisoo from 1941 to 1943. He was given this brief window of time.

Mr. Karrisoo, a tenor, had studied voice at Tartu Science School with La Signorina degli Abbati from 1931 to 1936. In an international singing competition in Vienna he won a silver medal. He also sang at the Vienna State Opera and the Royal Opera in Stockholm. Mr. Karisso was forced to flee for his life to Sweden in 1944.

Arno was able to study piano from Mrs. M. Schäfer. He had the opportunity to learn about the history of music, especially choral music, from Anton Kasemets, who had been the Artistic Director of the Estonian Opera. Besides being well-known as an organist, Mr. Kasemets also directed massed choirs at the Estonian Song Festivals.

Arno attended the Anna Torvand–Tellman's English College. He graduated in 1944 with an equivalent of Grade 13—a five year college preparatory program.

Estonia was experiencing the realities of war; the injustice, the humiliation and the fear. What had been a very good life became filled with the struggle to survive. The entire community became involved. Arno assisted those in his neighborhood by making sure the lights were out during blackouts, due to air-raids.

Arno's father watched as his son grew to manhood and saw there was intelligence and ambition in his nature.

Friedrich had been grooming him to follow in his footsteps and be a part of the prosperous hardware business. Arno would follow a very different path.

Arno's Story

Chapter Two

The Challenge of Darkness

Estonia was a gateway between Europe and Russia, with coasts on the Baltic Sea, the Gulf of Finland and the Gulf of Riga. The Baltic Sea was a vital trade route and fertile fishing ground for Estonia and the other nations that bordered the waterway. Countries realized the most crucial key to their military and economic success, or even keeping themselves alive, lay in their mastery of these ocean routes and the free approach and entry to their ports (Churchill).

This valuable arm of the North Atlantic Ocean was in trouble. Like many nations, Estonia had a history of foreign domination. Since the 12th century A.D. the nation faced wave after wave of occupiers; Denmark, Sweden, Germany, Poland, Russia, and the Soviet Union, all of which saw the strategic value of the area (The Singing Revolution). Small countries such as Estonia became pawns in various power struggles. The deadly comb ran back and forth and back again.

Estonia's darkest and bloodiest chapter began in 1940 when the Soviets crossed their border. Before that, nearly 90 percent of the people of Estonia were ethnic Estonians. After the Soviet takeover, under Stalin's rule, the Soviets tried to *russify* the nation by breaking up Estonian society. Russify is the term the Estonians used to describe this detestable process.

Within months thousands were executed, and many disappeared. They set out to accomplish this by imposing a system of mass deportations. On June 13 and 14, 1941, Soviet soldiers forcibly removed more than 10,000 Estonians from their homes. The deportees were sent to slave-labor camps in Siberia and other remote sections of the Soviet Union (Department, 1992). It was the educated, the wealthy and the prosperous which were targeted for deportation. This was done to break the spirit of the people and hinder them from resisting, making them feel helpless and hopeless.

The local Estonian community marks the Anniversary of the Estonian National Independence Day by sharing a meal at a restaurant and having someone speak about those days. Even after Arno's passing I continued to attend these gatherings.

On one of these occasions some of them, who were eyewitnesses of the horrors of those days, recounted their personal experiences. They told me how the men, women and children were torn from each other and herded like cattle into old, hot, stinking boxcars with locked doors. The windows were only narrow slits, some of which were barred with barbed wire. Imagine forty people crammed into such a small space.

My friend, Helgi Männiste, related how she would never forget the agony and anguish of the screams, the cries, the pleas and the begging from the cars with the children in them. Their little hands were outstretched at the side of the car where the door was slightly open. Helgi said, "The opening was not wide enough to push a loaf of bread through it."

They pleaded for someone to give them water. She had some food and she shouted at the Russian soldier to open the door and let her give them food and water. He had a rifle and could have shot her, but he didn't; instead he opened the door a little further so she could at least help that much. The weather was unbearably hot which increased the suffering. These scenes and sounds were etched on her memory.

She was also informed soldiers had been at her home looking for her. They had a list of names and her name was on it. She knew what was happening and hurried to her home, put a few necessities in a sheet, threw it over her shoulder–and ran!

Another couple, Elmar and Ebba Põldmaa, shared their story. He was then in the German army. He used a pole and shoved food through the narrow window bars of the cars to give the people something to eat. He did this at the risk of his life. He would have been shot if he had been caught. His wife had three soldiers pointing their guns at her, but she was able to escape. They both believe that angels protected them that day.

The book *Graves Without Crosses* by Arved Viirlaid describes the awful conditions that existed during this period of Estonian history. In the Preface to the book, John G. Diefenbaker (House of Commons, Ottawa, April 1972) wrote how this book describes the suffering of a group of people who are all too representative of millions who lived under the yoke of Communist dictatorship. "The things that happened to the Estonians are a reminder that history reveals: freedom dies when people take it for granted."

He also stated the author of this book has done well to emphasize the need for everyone to show by action and not by words alone a greater appreciation of freedom and a determination to guard it more vigilantly than ever before—the right to speak, the right to worship and the right to go about one's daily occupation without fear of arbitrary arrest.

Being sent to Siberia meant a slow death by starvation. What that would have been like is something I do not want even to imagine. During the cold of the Russian winter they were forced to labor there with nothing but vile, stinking water to drink and one crust of black bread to keep them alive.

The deadly odds were stacked against them. Their empty stomachs, the cold, and the brutality of the guards with the rifle was driving them like a herd of desperate, starving animals. It was a process, conditioning them so all their value as human beings was taken from them. They could not help but wonder what reason they still had to cling to life (Viirlaid, Graves Without Crosses, p. 76)–but they refused to give up!

Arno did not talk about those days but I have records of what he said when he was the one to speak at Estonian gatherings that describe in detail what he knew and how he felt.

He had a number of books in his library which I used in my research. *Estonia Then and Now* was one of the books. I read that just one week after the June 14th deportation, Germany staged an invasion. In doing so, they broke the Molotov-Ribbentrop Pact they had made with the Soviet Union; a pact in which the governments of the two countries would not attack, declare war or interfere in the activities of the other (Department, 1992).

At first, Estonians were relieved when the Nazis occupied their country and drove out the Soviets. However, Nazi rule was harsh. The Germans repeated the things the Russians had done, by arresting thousands of Estonians and sending them to slave-labor camps in Nazi-occupied Eastern Europe (Department, 1992, p. 35).

By 1944, the tide turned and Germany was losing the war. Russia returned with a vengeance. 100,000 Estonians fled to Sweden, Finland and Germany. Many of them drowned when the small boats and rafts they used to escape overturned in the rough waters. Many more vessels were sunk by Soviet airplanes and submarines (Department,

1992). This time the Soviets stayed for fifty years and nearly succeeded in eradicating Estonia.

After nearly 3,000 years living in their land, Estonians almost ceased to exist. What prolonged human tragedy these people suffered? What courage it has historically taken for them—to live on? Estonians resisted without resorting to guns. They fought with their voices. They fought and sang and survived (The Singing Revolution).

Arno's Story

Chapter Three

The Sounds and Horrors of War

Arno, now eighteen, was working for "Beton" A.G. Contractor as a Clerk-typist. He started working for them after graduation. Germany was in control of Estonia and Arno was conscripted. He was forced to sign a document stating he was a volunteer. If he had refused, he would have been imprisoned. The young men joked among themselves saying they were sent to the front "voluntarily against their will."

In September, 1944, Arno was stationed in Germany. On the front lines he found himself quickly engulfed in the business of war; the roar of tanks and planes, the blazing sound of guns and exploding bombs and the piercing, guttural cries of injured and dying mates. Permeating this was the nauseous stench of dead and decaying bodies.

So many of them--brave young men who had perished under the rubble of bombed buildings and enemy gunfire.

Arno was not prepared for these unspeakable horrors. Nothing in his entire realm of experience could have prepared him for such a graphic taste of a living hell. He was in a nightmare; scenes of dying and death his constant companions. Arno's inner conflict, the anguish, the mental and physical pain were overwhelming at times.

One day, in the thick of the battle, the bridge he was crossing was bombed. With shattered stones flying through the air, Arno lept off the bridge into the river below. When he landed in the water he struck a rock and broke his ankle. He struggled for two more days, limping on his injured ankle. He kept moving to evade discovery and certain death.

It was among the firefights and exploding shells Arno realized if he was ever going to come out of this war alive, only God could help him survive. Handling the indescribable terrors of war, and his own struggles with his fears and the chaos surrounding him, he needed the strength and hope only God could give. War illuminated realities about life and death which are incomprehensible under normal circumstances. War demonstrated the very worst and best of human nature.

Arno continued to hone his survival instincts. Near the end of the war he followed a battalion of tanks which broke through allied forces.

He knew if he delayed he would be trapped behind enemy lines and most likely be killed. This is a unique glimpse of the human spirit in action in Arno, and his will to survive against all odds.

Arno was one of the few men from his unit to survive that day. Once more God provided for him. I watched a program on TV about the remarkable things Jewish soldiers are doing today. They are using the skills acquired from their war experiences—skills hardwired into their minds. They are the skills necessary in order to survive. Some have been able to use these skills in amazing ways in their lives. I believe some of the special skills Arno had were a result of his wartime experiences.

After the war ended in 1945, Arno was interned in a refugee camp in Germany. The surviving young Estonian men who had been conscripted were in this camp of 16,000. They were exiles. Returning to Russian controlled Estonia would mean arrest, deportation to labour camps and almost certain death.

Arno kept a file of documents from his time in the camp. It gives a small glimpse of life there. For nine months he worked as an Interpreter at the U.S. Air Force, Cassel Air Base. A Temporary Base

Pass listed his age as 18, height: 6 ft. 1 inch, weight: 165 pounds, hair: blond, eyes: gray. He worked for the 493rd Air Service.

He was certified to drive a deuce-and-a-half (2 ½ ton) truck.   His 30th Infantry Employees Pass records his weight at 153 pounds when he was 19. He went from work in the morning back to the camp at night to sleep…if that was possible.

While working at I.R.O., at 908 Area Team Headquarters, in Hanover, he was given the position of Warehouse Manager.   He kept inventory and supervised dispensing of rations. When on duty he was permitted to wear Battle Dress and was permitted to travel in their vehicles during the course of his duties and getting to and from work. He also worked at two Displaced Persons Camps as the Chief Clerk, supervising camp offices and food stores.

His last position at the camps was at the camp post office in Fallingbostel, as chief clerk/investigator in the "Dead Letter Office." He supervised two clerks in redirecting mail to former inhabitants of the camp.

This was Arno's life for three years and eight months!

Left: Henry with
Mama and Papa
Below: Henry and
Arno

Above: Arno at eight.
Left: A family portrait

Clockwise from top :

The cottage at Pirita

Playing by the ocean

With Nanny Minnie

Mr. Opera!

Armanda degli Abbati   Mrs. M. Schäfer

Arno entertaining fellow students - 1934

Papa and Mama
Ambel

Left: Henry and his
fiancée Sigrid.

Chapter Four

The Light of a New Day

Arno immigrated to Canada in June 1949 with $10.00 in his pocket and an old grenade case which held all his earthly possessions. But he came with the dream of a better life.

He and his friend, Robert Timusk, crossed the ocean on the time-worn British liner "Samaria." Soon after leaving Germany they encountered a violent storm! Arno said it was so bad he thought their ship was going to go down. It was ironic to have survived the front lines and then face the possibility of drowning at sea.

They survived the storm and safely disembarked in Montreal, Quebec. They traveled by train to Carman, Manitoba, where jobs as farm hands waited for them, sponsored by the Manitoba Sugar Company.

Arno settled into Canadian living. He even acquired his Manitoba driver's license. But it didn't translate well on a practical level. His first task was to drive the tractor to plow the field. The goal was to plow a straight furrow. Fortunately there were other jobs on the farm which he was able to do.

He never did become a perfect driver. Most of the cars he operated ended up with a few dents and scrapes. Two of them were written off! It is a good thing his artistic abilities later opened up other avenues.

Even though they were under a contract, the work ran out. Because Arno's English was excellent he was chosen to go and negotiate with authorities. Work opportunities paved the way for him and the other workers to relocate to Sault Ste. Marie in October 1949.

The Ministry of Labor kept track of the workers who had come from the refugee camps. Arno received a certificate from the Deputy Minister of Labor, indicating he had faithfully fulfilled the undertaking which he was given before he departed Europe. He was to keep them informed when he moved or changed employment. This helped him when he applied for Canadian citizenship, which he received in 1956.

The countryside around Sault Ste. Marie is beautiful. This area was once rated among the twenty best places to live in Canada. It is to the hills, lakes and forests surrounding this picturesque northern town to which the "Group of Seven" were drawn time after time. This area inspired them to paint the pictures which made them famous. To Arno this northern landscape was more than just beautiful. In many ways it was similar to his beloved Estonia. It helped to soothe the ache in his heart for home.

Post war, soldiers were expected to simply pick up where they had left off and get on with life—easier said than done. No one knows what living in constant fear and stress does to a person unless one has experienced it. The soldiers dealt with violence and hate. They had psychological problems and suffered from post-traumatic stress syndrome. They experienced flash backs and were haunted by terrible memories. How could they forget what they had experienced? Often they could not and they were left to fight the inevitable pain, grief, anger and rage with no one to turn to.

Arno came through the war physically uninjured. Sadly he didn't escape the effects of the war unscathed.

His emotional, invisible wounds ran exceptionally deep—from which there was no escape. Someone once said, "Anger is like taking poison and expecting the other person to die." Anger issues from the past do not quietly evaporate when better times come. These unresolved issues would bring Arno to the brink of his endurance.

Arno and the Estonian people were pushed to the point of despair. They were inhumanly treated and devalued. Being demeaned like this by others is painful and strikes at ones self-respect.

Traumatic memories continued to haunt and torment Arno—many of his nights were interrupted by nightmares.

Arno's personal library had many books about the war, but he rarely talked about his experiences. Sometimes when watching a war movie he would become upset with the misrepresentations—he had been there and had lived through it.

Estonian friends who had escaped from Communist rule in Estonia told me when Arno first arrived in northern Ontario he was as thin as a coat rack. It took time for him to adjust to his new home. He struggled to earn a living. Compounded by memories left by the war, he faced a very real uncertainty of the future. He worked at Jardun Mines for a short time and then on a road repair crew before moving on to the Algoma Steel Corporation where he would spend the remainder of his working career.

Chapter Five

Building a New Life

Arno started the work of building a new life in Sault Ste. Marie. Looking back he would see the love and grace of God filling the dead places inside him with new life. He struggled to define the purpose of his own existence framed by his past. Having experienced the devaluation of who he was as an Estonian by the Communists and Nazis, he valued the freedom of the human spirit.

Desiring a deeper understanding of God, Arno turned to his religious roots. Less than one year after Arno's arrival in Canada, he was confirmed and then became a member of the Evangelical Lutheran Church. He played a significant role in the founding of the Estonian Evangelical Lutheran Church in Sault Ste. Marie in 1951. He was actively involved in the church, serving as president of the council for 24 years and as secretary for 18. He was also the church organist for fifty years. God and the church held a prominent place in his heart.

Arno worked to make sense of life and how he would live it. Armed with the knowledge God was there to turn to, he found a way to nourish his soul which would also benefit others. That way was through his knowledge of music and opera. It seemed to be an impossibility--an idea had so captured his imagination--he began to think anything was possible. Jack Canfield said, "Never let anyone tell you that something is not possible. God may have been waiting for centuries for someone ignorant enough of the impossible to do that very thing" (Canfield) .

Art creates a place where people from different cultures and backgrounds can come together and enjoy themselves. Musicians, writers and poets lay the ground work for society to show what people have in common, where people can get to know each other as human beings. There is power in music to heal the body, strengthen the mind and unlock the creative spirit (Campbell, 1997).

Arno's soul was exhilarated when circumstances opened opportunities for him to conduct choirs. He started conducting the Estonian Choir of Sault Ste. Marie in 1956, a position he held for eleven years. Besides being the organist at St. Marks for eight years, he also directed the church choir. Most of the works they sang were in German or Latin. He kept recordings of some of the special performances. Two of them, a Christmas program and a Springtime Cantata, were broadcast on the CJIC radio station. He was very busy during this time, serving as conductor of two choirs.

In 1966 he started conducting the Sault German-Austrian Centennial Choir. While with this choir he recorded *A Candlelight Cantata* and Christmas music for *Christmas Around the World*. Arno still had cassette tapes of the German-Austrian Choir. Their music was so beautiful to listen to! He conducted the group for five years.

While directing the German-Austrian Choir he also led the Zion Evangelical-Lutheran Church choir in 1968, for three years. Unlike the other choirs, which sang mostly in Estonian, German or Latin, this choir sang in English.

He even worked with the G. Marconi Italian Choir as conductor and arranger for three years. "I did not let them know I couldn't speak Italian," he told me in his typical humorous fashion.

He actively conducted choirs for over 24 years. Sometimes two or three at a time! This was in addition to his duties as a church organist—he often played at more than one church on a Sunday. When you include his fulltime job, later raising a family and everything else he was doing, he was one busy man!

His involvement in the arts extended to more than just music. He was a supporter and participant in many multicultural activities which included:

- Forming the Estonian Cultural Activities Committee connected with his Church in 1951, which later re-organized as the Estonian Association of Sault Ste. Marie.
- Cultural Events Coordinator of the Folk-Arts Council of Sault Ste. Marie, from 1964 to 1969.
- A Charter Member of the Allied Arts Council of Sault Ste. Marie, starting in 1968, and served as Vice-President of the Allied Arts Council of Sault Ste. Marie in 1982.
- A Founding Member of the Ontario Choral Federation in 1971.
- A Consulting Member of the Sault Symphony from 1982 - 1985.
- A member of the Ontario Advisory Board on Multiculturalism and Citizenship, from 1985 - 1987.

Not to mention achieving his personal goal of bringing opera to a hockey-mad steel town.

Chapter Six

Arno's Speech

When Arno was twenty nine years old, he was invited to speak at the 38th Anniversary of the Estonian National Independence Day. When he left Estonia twelve years earlier he had been cut off from all contact with his parents. Any attempt to reach out to them would have put their lives in danger. He had no way of knowing whether or not they survived the communist oppression of his home country. Likewise, they had no way of knowing if he was dead or alive. It would be another seven years before being reunited. What an emotional event!

The thoughts he expressed, the intensity of his feelings, and the depth of his concern for the plight of his fellow countrymen are evident in what he said that day. He spoke about the courage of his people and the need to promote dignity and respect for mankind. It is the history of his people. He delivered his speech in Estonian. The following excerpt is a translation:

"38 years ago today, on the 24th of February, a small and courageous nation regained for a short period of time its independence, which it had lost to its powerful invading neighbors 700 years ago. For 3,000 years the Estonians have been living on the shores of the Baltic Sea in the northeast corner of Europe.

"They enjoyed national freedom until the 13th century, but from that time on they were governed by a succession of foreign rulers, culminating in the conquest of the Estonian territory by Czarist Russia in 1710. Even though they became a part of the vast Russian empire, this country still remained an outpost of western culture.

"It was the policy of the Russian government to oppress the Estonian national culture by great russification programs, during the height of which, in the years 1888-89, even the children were forbidden to talk in their own language while attending public schools.

"These policies failed to subdue the national spirit of the Estonians. Instead the nationalist movements grew. They were spurred on by the common desire of the whole nation and, by the time of World War I, they were demanding an autonomous status for Estonia.

"The opportunity for the Estonians to realize their aspirations came with the fall of the czarist regime in Russia. While the Great Russian Empire was falling apart in the chaos of revolution, the Estonian National Council proclaimed Estonia an independent nation on February 24, 1918. On that date they stated that– 'as of today Estonia, within its historical and ethnic boundaries, is proclaimed an independent, democratic republic.'

"Independence, though, was not won in such an easy manner. Invading forces of the Russian Communist army and a mercenary force of demobilized German soldiers of the beaten Kaiser's army, in the pay of the 'Baltic Barons,' former big estate owners of German origin in the Estonian territory, had to be repelled. Estonia hastily organized its military defense.

"Although fighting on two fronts and greatly outnumbered by its opponents, the young Estonian Army proved its worth on the battlefield, each soldier spurred on by the ideal of freedom for his country. In June 1919 the German forces were scattered and on February 2, 1920 the peace treaty with the Soviets was concluded. By this treaty Soviet Russia renounced 'voluntarily and forever all rights of sovereignty formerly held by Russia over the Estonian people and territory.'

"As usual, there was a lack of good faith on the part of the Soviets. Even before the treaty was signed, the following report appeared in the official Soviet newspaper, *Izvestia*, on January 28, 1920: 'Comrade Lenin answered a question about the terms of peace with Estonia.' He said, 'We do not want to shed the blood of workers and Red Army soldiers for the sake of a piece of land, especially since this concession is not forever.'

"The Estonians, keeping a watchful eye on their neighbor in the east, set about to build up their war-ravaged economy on a self-sustaining basis. Industrial reorganization based on domestic raw materials was achieved and oil-shale mining became the biggest industry in the country. Important positions were occupied also by the light mechanical and electrical industries, the lumber and wood pulp industry, and the food industry. Increased production in agriculture as a result of land reform enabled the country to export agricultural products on a large scale and the country became prosperous with a flourishing economy.

"Estonians constituted 88.2% of Estonia's total population of 1,133,917. The national minorities were Russians, Germans, Jews, Swedes and Latvians, all of which enjoyed special protection under the Estonian constitution. They were allowed to organize their own autonomous schools, cultural and welfare institutions.

"Estonia was predominantly a Lutheran country, although there was no established church. About 78.2% of the population belonged to this denomination and 19% to the Greek Orthodox Church. Elementary education was free and compulsory. An adequate number of state or municipal secondary schools prepared pupils for universities. The National University at Tartu soon became a widely recognized center of study and research. A number of museums, libraries, and other cultural institutions enriched the life of the nation.

"At the outbreak of World War II Estonia, together with its Baltic neighbors (Latvia and Lithuania) struggled to remain neutral. A guarantee of the independence of the Baltic States was on the agenda of the Anglo-French-Soviet negotiations in the summer of 1939.

"The Soviet Union, however, had been secretly negotiating with Hitler and on August 23, 1939, signed a non-aggression treaty, the so-called Ribbentrop-Molotov Pact. In a secret protocol, Finland, Estonia, and Latvia were placed within the Soviet sphere of influence.

"This gave the Soviet Union a free hand in its dealings with Estonia, notwithstanding all previous treaties and agreements. The consequences of the Ribbentrop-Molotov Pact were soon to be felt in Estonia. Within a month, Russia bludgeoned the Baltic States into granting military bases to Soviet troops on their territory, all the while promising not to interfere with their internal affairs.

"During the winter 1939-40 the next victim, Finland, was beaten into submission, and having obtained more bases, Russia proceeded to the 'second phase of consolidating its Baltic flank.' This took place from June 15 to 17, 1940, when Zhdanov, Vkyshinsky and Dekanozov, posing as 'diplomatic couriers,' flew into the Baltic capitals and in well-rehearsed operation, executed with the aid of Soviet troops stationed in the Baltic States, arranged for local stooges to take over.

"Fake elections were held and communist-dominated parliaments established. These were ordered to apply for the incorporation of the Baltic States into the Soviet Union. With this began one of the greatest tragedies of modern human history. The Soviet occupants started the slow extermination of the Estonian, Latvian and Lithuanian nations.

"The terror under the first Soviet occupation of the Baltic republics reached its zenith with the deportation of June 14, 1941. The majority of deportees were the most ordinary workers and farmers, whose only crime was their national origin. There were children in arms and very old people, barely able to walk. This caused the Estonians, Latvians and Lithuanians for the first time to think the ultimate aim of the Soviets might be the annihilation of the Baltic nations. Subsequent events confirmed these apprehensions.

"During the first Soviet occupation from 1940-41 Estonia lost 53,547 inhabitants or 6.7 per cent of the entire population. They were murdered, deported or arrested. If the same figure would be applied to Canada, this country would have lost percentage-wise over 900,000 inhabitants. However, the destruction of the Baltic nations did not end in 1941, when the Russians were driven from the Baltic countries by the advancing German armies. The Germans stayed in Estonia for three years and drained the country of its last resources. Then, in 1944, the Russians returned and darkness closed in for good.

"For a brief moment in 1944, as the Germans were evacuating the country, Estonian patriots tried to organize an utterly hopeless resistance against the advancing Russian forces, using arms left behind by the Germans or forcing the retreating German soldiers to surrender their arms to them, but the Estonian tricolor waved only for a few days over the nation's capital and the desperate resistance movement was crushed by the attacking Russian army. 'Information which since then has penetrated the Iron Curtain tells of recurrent waves of arrests, both of individuals and whole families.'

"Scurrying trucks with mysterious loads and armed MVD guards in the night, people being awakened with rifle butts and trains of cattle cars with barred windows on the siding of some station are everyday realities in the Baltic States. The deportations were renewed on an even larger scale. According to the data, the deportations in Estonia, between 1946 and 1949, by far exceeded the one in 1941. In Latvia approximately 70,000 persons were deported after 1944 and in Lithuania the six major deportation waves after 1944 netted nearly 15 per cent of the total population.

"World opinion has been curiously oblivious of the fate of the Baltic countries. It seems somehow to be taken for granted that they must be sacrificed for the benefit of the rest of mankind. It does not seem to be the correct thing to take any notice of their desperate plight.

"Nevertheless the Estonians, like the Latvians and the Lithuanians, still hold out. They still fail to believe that active, progressive, civilized and peaceful nations can be simply thrown on the scrap heap.

"They still await the day when all Estonians, Latvians, Lithuanians–both those still in the country and those who are displaced, dispersed and deported–are enabled to express their will in a really free and democratic way, uninitiated by the presence of the forces of an alien tyranny. Then they will be able to make these contributions to the Western democratic civilization of which they have shown themselves to be capable. This is the least they are entitled to expect.

"There are about two hundred people of Estonian origin living in the Sault today, many of them escapees of those fateful days of 1944. They consider themselves fortunate to have broken free of the Red yoke and now enjoy a way of life they love most in a country which has welcomed them with open arms and offered them an opportunity to re-establish themselves as New Canadians. It is an opportunity which they have thankfully accepted and learned to appreciate and follow; the Canadian way of life.

"They cannot forget the fate of their unhappy countrymen who had to stay behind, and the injustice being done to the country of their birth.

"And if they pause in their everyday work to commemorate the day when their native country shed the yoke of foreign rule, should they be reminded they should forget about the past and concentrate on adjusting themselves to their present environment?

"It is the cultural heritage of many nations, beginning with Cartier, Champlain and Wolfe, that has forged Canada into the great nation which it is today.

"The Estonian immigrants, while trying to become good Canadians, still retain some of the customs and traditions they have been brought up with, and so offer their share to be added to the great cultural heritage of the nations that founded this country. To quote Bruce Hutchinson, the great Canadian historian and novelist: 'A human being has felt the immemorial tug of his own soil, people and history. He would be a poor human being if he didn't.'

"And so we wish to the future Canadians of Estonian extraction, that they might yet see the day, when their brothers in their old home country will regain their independence and rejoin the ranks of the free nations of the world."

The same day Arno spoke these words to his fellow countrymen, a program he had organized was aired on the local radio stations, CKCY and CJIC, commemorating the observance of the Estonian National Independence Day. Music was a focal point of the program and it began with an adaptation of an old Estonian folk song.

In 1960, Arno did an 8" by 11" charcoal drawing of Tallinn and entered it in a contest. It won a special award. To say it is really well done does not do it justice. The place of his birth was always close to his heart. The spires of St. Olaf's Church are visible in the drawing. It was the tallest building in the world between 1549 and 1625.

The picture still has a prominent position hanging over the piano in my living room.

Celebrating Estonian Heritage

The Sault Ste. Marie Estonian community would gather at their lodge to celebrate their heritage during the 1960s.

Tallinn by Arno Ambel

Chapter Seven

Arno and Vilma's Wedding

Arno married Vilma Kahu on November 23, 1961. The ceremony took place at St. Mark's Evangelical Lutheran Church. The choir that he normally conducted honored them by singing a wedding hymn. It was the union of two talented people with a vision–both having a passion for music. I doubt even they could have imagined what they would eventually accomplish. Their contribution of music was to have a significant impact on the cultural evolution of Sault Ste. Marie.

Vilma was born in Otepaa, Estonia. She began singing publicly at the age of three when her father stood her on a table and told her to sing. Her father and sister were amateur actors and she had a brother who was a professional violinist. She was in every school play and in her church choir as well. From her youth Vilma loved opera. Then her career was interrupted by the war (Waples, Starlite, 1982).

Vilma came to Canada in 1949. She was an energetic, fun loving person with a beautiful voice.

She was often a soloist in the choirs Arno directed. She had two sons, Peter, who now lives in Mering, Germany, and Toomas who lives in Windsor, Ontario.

Arno and Vilma participated in an Allied Arts Summer Festival concert. The German Choir sang under Arno's leadership and Vilma sang in the choir. It was noted in the Sault Star that they received the best applause of the evening (July 6, 1962).

Negotiations began in 1962 to arrange for Arno's parents, Rudolf Friedrich and Liisu-Lisbeth to come to Canada. Getting out of the Soviet-occupied country was not easy. This was made possible by the local branch of the Red Cross Missing Persons Committee. They overcame many obstacles in obtaining the necessary permission for them to emigrate.

The danger they faced was very real. Arno told me of an incident concerning his father and the cloud of suspicion and mistrust which shrouded their lives. Friedrich owned a transmitter radio. The KGB (Russian Secret Police) learned about it and suspected he was a spy.

One of Friedrich's friends was an officer in the Russian army. He discovered the KGB's plans to arrest and probably execute him. Friedrich's friend went to visit him. When the police arrived and saw a Russian officer at the apartment they saluted, apologized and left.

After nineteen years apart the family finally reunited in 1963. The Sault Star reported the reunion that morning at the airport. His parents seemed anxious and hesitant as they walked down the stairs from the plane to begin a new life in freedom. Doubts quickly vanished. Arno broke from the small delegation of flower-carrying countrymen and raced to greet them.

Mama Ambel was profuse with kisses, tears, talking and hugging. The moment she had dreamed about for nearly two decades had arrived. Overcome with joy she spoke in a combination of Estonian, German and English, "I am glad to be here!"

Papa Ambel, more reserved, greeted Arno with a polite, but firm handshake and a buzz on both cheeks.

The picture which appeared with the story showed a young Reet Kaldma wearing traditional Estonian dress, presenting a gift of flowers to Mama Ambel.

Two days before, the elder Ambels said good-bye forever to their friends and relatives in Tallinn. Their journey commenced in Moscow, via London, then Toronto and finally Sault Ste. Marie. Mama Ambel described the flight. "It was just wonderful."

It was the first time she had been aboard an aircraft. The only delay in their journey was by customs officials in Toronto. They ended up spending the night there before completing the last leg of their journey.

Mama and Papa Ambel started the work of settling in to their new life in Canada. They had found an apartment and were preparing to move into it when Friedrich passed away on December 16, 1963. The conditions under which they had been living for 24 years and the strain of the move, took their toll on his health. He lived here in freedom for only six months. Arno and Vilma decided it would be best if Mama lived with them.

The family grew again when they welcomed their son, Frederick Henry, on March 17, 1966. Mama Ambel was delighted to have a grandson to love and help in his care.

The Ambels were also involved in a special Dominion Day Celebration that year. Now called

Canada Day, July 1st marked the day when Queen Victoria granted Canada its independence as a nation.

Sault Ste. Marie, Ontario shares a border with Sault Ste. Marie, Michigan, separated by the Ste. Mary's River. The United States celebrates their Independence Day on July 4th. The newly formed Folk Arts Association worked with their American counterparts to co-ordinate activities and created an international celebration. Arno was the Cultural Coordinator for the Association (Curran, June 29, 1966).

Nine ethnic groups participated in a three-hour concert at Bellevue Park's outdoor Band shell and an adjacent stage which was added for the venue. About 240 Sault residents of European descent dressed in their national costumes participated in the event. Arno directed a mixed choir of Ukrainian, German-Austrian and Estonians.

The festivities were opened by Mayor Alex Harry. He accepted flags which represented the various ethnic groups, Ontario, Canada and the U.S. The festivities, which attracted over 4,000 people included the concert, a military jet fly-by and a fireworks display ignited on a barge in the Ste. Mary's River. Throughout the weekend there were games, athletic events, drama, song, and folk dancing. The celebrations ended with the American Independence Day fireworks.

This was the first official event conducted by the Folk Arts Association which represented twenty-five ethnic groups.

Mr. Opera!

Arrival at Montreal
Arno and a friend at the international border
Confirmation at St. Marks

Vilma Ambel

The long-awaited family reunion

Some of the Choirs Arno has worked with.

Mr. Opera!

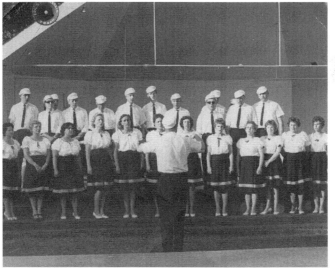

This last choir is the Zion Lutheran Choir which Arno and I sang in .

Arno's Story

Chapter Eight

Opera for a Steel Town

Arno and Vilma became involved in theatre when they joined the Musical Comedy Guild. An excellent start for Arno, he played the part of Émile de Becque, the male lead, in Rodgers and Hammerstein's *South Pacific*.

The Ambels made friends quickly. They were disappointed, however, with the Guild's lack of interest in opera productions. Although the Guild had performed works by Gilbert and Sullivan, Lehar and Strauss in the past, by 1969 the consensus was to concentrate on Broadway-type musical productions.

Some opera buffs in the area started thinking there was enough talent in the city to attempt a shot at mounting a full scale opera. They formed an organization which would become known as the Sault Opera Society.

Arno, Wilf Beauchamp and Ed Gartshore started the ball rolling and commenced pre-production work on Mozart's classic masterpiece,

The Marriage of Figaro. Arno wrote the forward for the program:

"A new venture for Sault Ste. Marie, the first locally produced classical opera, is ready for presentation for 'trial and judgment' to you, our fellow citizens of Sault Ste. Marie. Will there be enough of you coming to see it to make it financially feasible? Will the quality of our performance be on a standard high enough to justify the effort of an amateur group to produce a work which is generally regarded as a masterpiece of classical operatic literature? And finally, will you enjoy the presentation of a comedy set to music in the classical operatic style? It is a gamble in which we must get a passing grade, on all three counts, to justify our venture."

It took a lot of courage to risk undertaking such an adventure. Financial backing was provided by the local German-Austrian Centennial Choir. Arno took on the task of directing and producing the opera. The group recruited a 34-voice chorus and 22-piece orchestra. The Korah Collegiate Auditorium was chosen for the venue. The Musical Comedy Guild and Sault Theatre Workshop supplied costumes and flats for stage sets. Many of their membership worked on the production crew.

Robin Waples, entertainment critic for the Sault Star, looked back on that evening in an article. She wrote:

"It was a cold winter's night in February when some 200 people trudged through the snow to witness the Sault's first locally mounted production of a grand opera, Mozart's *The Marriage of Figaro*. A crowd of 200 was not a bad showing for a city that traditionally was more interested in hockey than in classical music, let alone opera. They only lost $80.00 on this first production and they were delighted. It was quite an achievement. That was proof enough to Arno that there was an audience for opera in the Sault, the wilds of the north-country" (September 9, 1996).

Arno wore many hats for the production. Not only was he the producer, he also served as the choirmaster, set designer and played Bartolo. Vilma played Countess Almaviva. Her beautiful voice and wonderful sense of humor only added greatly to the enchanted evening.

The Society's first President was Ted LaBerge. Arno served as Vice President in charge of productions (and stage director for its next productions), and Samuel Bessant was the Music Director.

The Organization's second production, Strauss's *The Gypsy Baron*, was a greater financial success than the first: It broke even. The Sault Opera's early successes caused some debate in the small theatre community. There were concerns the fledgling company would affect their income in competing for entertainment dollars and a small audience pool. Arno didn't let his critics get to him. His thought on the topic was competition kept standards high. He said, "You have to be lean and hungry to accomplish something."

Arno had high expectations. He understood he was never going to please everyone—that every person was not going to like him—that is just the way it is—nor would they agree with the vision he had.

Arno believed taking risks propels our life into a new level of adventure: like walking on a tightrope. Learning such a feat requires skill, discipline and perseverance. It does not just happen. Arno's leap into opera involved tremendous risk and many obstacles such as the possibility of failure. It was a roller coaster ride of a balancing act. As Arno discovered he needed God in the midst of war, he knew he needed to look to God for this venture's success.

Arno said: "Right from the beginning, we said (Arno and Vilma) we'd either commit ourselves fully or not at all. We take what we do seriously, and we hope that the group is going to grow into something which can be regarded as a semi-professional opera company."

It was obvious whether his dream came true or not he would always be devoted to opera. Growing a successful opera company was not an easy task but he and Vilma had committed themselves to the task. Several of Arno's acquaintances said his contributions to the Society were made with all the care and devotion a father would give to his newborn son.

Arno applied the same passion to the Opera Society as he put into any of his endeavors. He aimed for the highest standard they could achieve for a show and held the cast to the same expectations. He broke more than one baton in his enthusiasm to get it just right.

The Ambels built much laughter and fun into their lives. Although "Laughter is the best medicine," is an old cliché, Arno and Vilma found it to be true. There was much pain and sorrow for those who had lived through the war or suffered similar hardships. They had a need to be able to laugh.

Arno chose operas we would call feel-good productions. They were chosen to lift the spirit and nourish the soul. Laughter, music and nature divert our attention from difficulties.

Arno and Vilma discovered other benefits from their involvement in the theater. Being in a musical production or in a choir was like being in a large extended family, you get to know people and they become a part of your life. Relationships are built with the people around you—it is heart to heart. In the theatre you need, want and enjoy a variety of personalities. You accept them for who they are, with their attributes and with their flaws. You accept them for the good things they bring to your life and forget about the rest. Every person involved becomes an important part of the production—each individual brings something unique.

Singing benefits us in a way nothing else can. It is an expression of the soul. Music is a powerful vehicle for delivering hope and healing.

Top left: Arno and Vilma painting sets in their living room - 1971
Vilma as Countess Almaviva in *The Marriage of Figaro*
Arno with Isobel Tugwell Quonta Film festival Best Director 1983 and Vilma for costume design

Vilma with Son Fred in *The King and I*. Arno conducting for *The Mikado* and (below) Arno as Zorba with Will Gartshore.

Sault Opera: Zorba 1993 2004.10 Scrapbook 55 Courtesy of Sault Ste. Marie Public Library (ssmpl.ca)

Arno's Story

Chapter Nine

More About Sault Opera

Sault Opera surveyed the public as well as their own members for their third production in 1971. The winner was *The Student Prince,* by Romberg. The troupe and the audience enjoyed the performance. Sault Opera even turned a profit!

Sault Opera mounted a production of *Carmen* the following spring. The group was able to obtain federal and provincial training grants which helped with the company's financial challenges. Through Arno's efforts, Sault Opera was chartered as an Ontario Non-profit Corporation, and was registered as a federally approved charitable organization. That autumn, they produced the classic, *Don Giovanni.*

With the help of another grant, Arno and Vilma organized a Wardrobe and Costume Rental Department. Robin Waples wrote an article in the Starlight that tells about this project. Prior to this venture, Vilma didn't know what a sewing machine was. Budgets were tight to produce shows and they learned to do everything themselves to save money. She used Mother Ambel's sewing machine and with all the how-to books she could find she learned this new craft by reading and doing. She progressed to designing her own costumes and enjoying the creative challenge (Wap82).

Audiences loved her work too and in 1975 Vilma received a Quanta Regional Drama Festival Award for her designs for *Helen Goes to Troy*. Arno won the director's prize that same year.

Their home became Sault Opera's headquarters. A spare room became a Sault Opera office. Often their living room was used to paint the sets and their dining room served as the costume department. When producing the *Gypsy Baron*, they ate off of trays for months. "But they loved it," Vilma said. Often there would be a half-sewn costume slung over a living room chair or an open book of period costumes lying on the coffee table. Costumes were stored in the basement and props in the back yard and the garage. The blocking of shows was paced out in the living room. This is a picture of their home at that time.

Arno had a good knowledge of history and he insisted that the costumes had to be just right for the period. That was his way of looking at it.

Eventually the basement housed 650 costumes, 30 pairs of 'character' shoes, numerous hats, umbrellas, canes, wigs, swords, jewelry, and anything else that had been or could be used in a Sault Opera production.

By the 1980's Sault Opera had the largest and best-equipped theatrical wardrobe in Northern Ontario. Vilma was well-known as a costume designer and seamstress. Her long hours of work and personal sacrifice did pay off. She had a number of friends who worked long hours with her. She found their help invaluable.

They were able to earn additional income by renting out costumes to other theatre companies in northern Ontario and Michigan as well as individuals. On Halloween as many as 400 costumes were rented out to party-goers.

After the closing of the production of the operetta *The Great Waltz*, the company was facing financial difficulties. Following much discussion the organization adopted a policy whereby a popular musical show, such as a Broadway-type musical or other, would be performed whenever financially necessary. This should guarantee better box office receipts in order to cover foreseeable losses of classical opera or operetta productions.

It seems many Broadway musicals were written by Jewish song writers. These writers had lived with racial intolerance and persecution like Arno had. Much of their work contained comedy and a message of hope—we can and will survive. Even though opera came first with Arno, I think these musicals would have touched him deeply.

The Sound of Music was cast in the summer of 1973 and performed in January. Vilma once again played a leading role. This production was a "first" for Arno producing, designing, and directing both the music and staging of the show. It was a box office and artistic success.

They quickly followed up with a production of the opera *Martha* in the spring of 1974, and *The King and I* in the fall. They followed a similar pattern in future seasons, a musical and then an opera or operetta.

They performed the rock opera *Jesus Christ Superstar* in the fall of 1975. Sault Opera was the first theatre group to perform the musical in Canada.

Before the production of the musical *Gigi*, in 1979, the company relied upon local talent for filling the lead parts of its productions. The major leads in most of the shows had made Sault Opera into the popular theatre organization it had become.

In order to balance the lead ensembles, especially in future opera performances, they decided to start hiring professional artists if necessary. Arno believed there was enough talent in the Sault to put on good musicals, but classic operas demanded specially-trained voices. There were not enough classically-trained opera singers in Sault Ste. Marie available. Arno's work behind-the-scenes allowed the company to pursue highly talented professionals to work on the shows and train local people in their various areas of expertise.

Opera productions usually attract smaller audiences than the Broadway-type musicals. Arno never gave up hope people would give serious opera a try. He said, "If we could only get all those who come to the popular musicals to come and see the classical works, then we'd have half the battle won. They'd realize that classic opera can be just as entertaining and amusing as anything else." This was the lesson he learned as a child.

Arno scheduled his vacation time at Algoma Steel around Sault Opera's production schedules. He spent many hours getting a show ready for opening night, always aiming for the highest standard he could achieve. "We could put on smaller productions," he said, "But I wanted to present shows using all the resources available. I like to do full-scale productions with full crew, full cast, and full orchestra. It's good to have lots of people involved." As president of Sault Opera, Arno stressed the importance of upgrading the company "even if it means kicking me in the butt and getting someone better." He was always striving for excellence.

The Magic Flute was performed in June of 1979. It became a great artistic success and proved to be the milestone of the Opera's hopes.

Robin Waples, of the Sault Star, wrote many articles about Sault Opera's productions. The headline on this one reads, "Audience gives *Student Prince* a standing ovation. Sault Ste. Marie's theatre season couldn't end on a more pleasing note than with Sault Opera's engaging production of the classic light opera, *The Student Prince*. It was warmly received by an appreciative audience. The standing ovation that followed the three-hour production was well deserved. Producer, director, designer, (just one of those roles is a daunting task) Arno, and assistant director and choreographer Stephen Rutti assembled a talented cast that worked well together and looked happy. Comedy came in the form of the prince's pompous valet Lutz, portrayed haughtily by Stephen Rutti, and the domineering mother of Princess Margaret, Grand Duchess Anastasia, played to the hilt by Vilma. The large cast appeared well organized, relaxed, and as if they were enjoying what they were doing." (Waples, 1981)

The headline for another article Robin wrote announced: "Driving force, Ambel is Sault's Mr.

Opera." Following this praise she wrote: "Arno Ambel thinks he's mellowing. He hasn't broken a baton in two seasons. The Sault Opera musical conductor, who's been known to crack a baton or two in his enthusiasm, feels he's toning things down. Don't you believe it. Arno Ambel has been the driving force behind the local opera company since its inception in 1970, and there's no reason to think he's going to stop driving now…As a conductor, Ambel never looked back." "I guess I've put more effort into Sault Opera than anything else," he said with obvious pride. (Waples, Driving Force, Ambel is Sault's Mr. Opera, February 20, 1982)

Something had happened in Sault Ste. Marie—people discovered Sault Opera, and a new standard of musical theatre. Sault Ste. Marie was a mill town. The critics said it couldn't be done. It WAS done, and it lasted for 29 years until Arno's declining health made it impossible for him to continue to be a driving force behind it. Even productions with $40,000-to-$50,000 budgets made money in this hockey-mad steel town. Arno had accomplished the impossible. (Waples, September 9, 1996)

When Arno received the Medal of Merit, which is the city's most prestigious honor, an article in the Theatre Ontario News reported:
"Arno Ambel, President and founding member of the Sault Opera Society, was recently hon-

ored by the City of Sault Ste. Marie with the 1983 Medal of Merit. Mr. Ambel was presented with the award for his outstanding contribution to the community over a number of years and for his leadership of the Sault Opera Society."

In a newspaper article in the Sault Star, regarding the award, it read, "He has done much to develop talent in the Sault by giving those with musical or theatrical ability a chance to perform." (December 31, 1983)

Arno was the Stage Director of 20 of Sault Opera's 60 musical stage productions, Music Director and Conductor of 32 of these productions—as well as being actively involved in the production work to bring the plays to stage. Arno served on Sault Opera's Board of Directors for 26 years. He spent 10 years as Vice President in charge of productions—and a total of 13 as the president of the organization until he stepped down from the executive in 1996. He continued to act as consultant for the new production people for a further three years, and finally retired as a Board member in September of 1999.

Vilma's sudden death in April 1983 devastated Arno. In a memoriam he wrote about his wife: "Vilma Ambel was a founding member of The Sault Opera Society; a lead performer in 14 of Sault Opera's stage productions, founder, designer and supervisor of the wardrobe department; Member of the Board of Directors of Theatre Ontario, and posthumous co-recipient of the Medal of Merit of the City of Sault Ste. Marie." The award, which was presented on January 7, 1984, was inscribed to both Arno and Vilma. He also wrote, "I've always leaned on her. We worked things out together."

In their efforts to promote the arts, he acknowledged he could not have succeeded in doing what he did without her encouragement and help. Vilma's support was extremely valuable to him. After her death he stopped writing about the history of Sault Opera.

Arno had a heart attack in June 1985. Upon his cardiologist's advice he took an early retirement. A certificate he received commended him for 33 years and nine months of loyal and faithful service to the Algoma Steel Corporation.

Arno was also the curator of Sault Opera Archives. They are currently housed in the Archive Department at the Sault Ste. Marie Public Library. They are preserved in a humidity and temperature controlled environment and are available to the public whenever they might wish to see them.

Arno's Story

Chapter Ten

Singing Pigs and Other Stories

Arno kept many files about his involvement in the arts here in the Sault. He wrote a short history of Sault Opera recording the events that took place from 1969 until Vilma's death. He wrote: "A lot of interesting events can happen in 15 years of existence! Here are some fascinating 'highlights' of those years!"

- The media made a big fuss when the public auditions for *The Gypsy Baron* included a piglet. Not just any piglet but one "...which had to oink in the key of G Major." The animal was to oink in time with the pig-farming character Zsupan during one of his couplets.

  The star was found and named *Arnold*, after its thespian namesake for the old T.V. show *Green Acres* and in homage to the director, Arno. The pig's name was changed to *Salome* after it was discovered he was a she.

- A stagehand, the male lead and the entire pit orchestra were almost asphyxiated by an overzealous smoke machine during the technical rehearsals of *Don Giovanni*. The machine was not used after that.

- The director performed an emergency tune up on a grand piano with a monkey wrench in Newberry, Michigan. The piano exacted its revenge when one of the legs broke during the performance and ended up in the lap of the accompanist. Fortunately the frame supporting the foot pedals prevented serious injury.

- Blair House, who played Figaro in the 1980 production of *The Barber of Seville* announced at 10 a.m. on the day of the Friday performance he had lost his voice. With the help of the Actors' Equity a new Figaro had been found by 1:30. The actor, pulled out from under his kitchen sink doing a plumbing job, didn't even have time to shave before he was rushed to the airport and landed in Sault Ste. Marie at 2:30.

  When he arrived we discovered he was not familiar with our version of the English translation. However, after a few quick rehearsals, he sight-read and sang it perfectly from the orchestra pit. The voiceless Figaro lip-synched the part on stage.

- During opening night of *The Merry Wives of Windsor* a member of the chorus stepped off a seven foot riser and fell into the orchestra pit. He lay unconscious for twenty minutes while being attended to by a doctor in the audience who had witnessed the fall.

  The actors playing Falstaff and Mr. Ford, unaware of the accident, carried on their duet without missing a beat. They were understandably disappointed with the lack of audience reaction to their performance.

The mystery was solved when they saw the paramedics wheeling the man out of the theatre on a gurney. He returned to the production two days later, but was re-assigned to a different position on the stage.

- During the first 15 years of Sault Opera's existence, eight couples met and married who were members of the cast, orchestra or production crew. Maybe there is something special in finding your mate in the hubbub of activity that goes on during a musical theatre production.

Arno's Story

Chapter Ten

Freedom, A People's Dream

Although Arno was busy with Sault Opera, his heart was still strongly connected to his beloved Estonia. The search for news of what was happening "back home" was very important to him. In the 80's hope and excitement began to build.

The Soviet government expected the people's desire for a free Estonia to weaken, because so many native Estonians were living outside of their homeland. The Russians would learn differently.

The struggle for independence gained momentum in 1985 when Mikhail Gorbachev became leader of the Soviet Union. He relaxed the restrictions on religion, language and movement within Estonia. On August 23, 1987, thousands of demonstrators gathered in Tallinn to denounce the Molotov-Ribbentrop Pact on its 48th anniversary. In the following year, Estonian activists created the Estonian National Independence party; the first opposition party to form openly in the Soviet Union (Estonia Then and Now, p. 37).

Throughout history, Estonians preserved their culture and national identity through song-fests, writings, religious gatherings and traditional festivals. Beginning in 1869, every five years, people from all over Estonia gathered to sing in a song festival called "Laulupida." This festival united the nation in the face of foreign occupiers for more than a century.

These celebrations kindled and fortified the courage to express their love of language and nation, and their reluctance to be absorbed by anyone. The festivals were a nationwide phenomenon. The power of the human voice collectively gathered together in song enabled them to overcome oppression (The Singing Revolution).

Years later, the Jubilee Song and Folk-Dance Festival of 1969 was attended by 30,230 performers and an audience of 200,000. Unforgettable displays of colorful Estonian national costumes worn by the singers and dancers added to the occasion (German, Merelinn Tallinn, p. 46).

In 1988 Soviet tanks surrounded the grounds at the Estonian Song Festival while the Estonians sang about the deep love of their country and their hope for freedom.

The fall of the Berlin Wall in 1989 marked the beginning of the end of the Soviet Union. All the countries occupied by the Soviet Union dreamed about freedom. In January 1989, the Estonian legislature declared Estonian, not Russian, would be the country's official language.

It is often simple things God uses to accomplish His purposes. On August 23, 1989, more than one million people from the Baltic States linked hands in a human chain that stretched from Tallinn, Estonia to Latvia's capital, Riga, to Vilnius, Lithuania, a distance of 400 miles (Estonia Then and Now, p. 38). They stood shoulder-to-shoulder, quietly, to show the world the ultimate injustice done to them for half a century by the Soviet Union (Männiste, 2008).

The Estonians waged a non-violent war. A nation of barely one million people, half a million foreign settlers and 100,000 Soviet troops, could not threaten the Soviet Union militarily or economically, so it had to do it with the force of its culture. The Estonians were able to win freedom for their country by singing.

Music sustains, transforms and binds people together. The force of the human voice massed in song was the cultural catalyst that energized, awoke and united the Estonians. It was called the Singing Revolution, the bloodless but powerful force that helped Estonia break from the crumbling Soviet Union. Estonia sang its way to freedom. They were united and singing when their country was being invaded and not a single person was killed (The Singing Revolution, 2006).

On August 20, 1991, the Estonian Supreme Council met in the Parliament building on Toompea, in Tallinn and proclaimed Estonia an independent republic. Their suffering and long years of hardship and horror, was largely unknown or overlooked by many countries. Most had not recognized the Soviet Union's occupation of Estonia and the other Baltic states.

The silence of this era masked the murder of twenty million people under Soviet control (Pfeiffer, Human Edge, Facing the Dead, 2005). These people were considered enemies of the state. Even to own a photograph of those who had been killed was punishable by death. Photographs were retouched and doctored, wiping out any trace that these people ever existed (Pfeiffer). The extreme hardship of the Stalinist era is beyond our comprehension, but it is oh so real to those who lived through it.

When Estonia declared its independence, more than 40 countries confirmed and congratulated them. In this moment of triumph, the joy of their victory was overwhelming!

There are no words to describe how happy this news made Arno and the Estonians. Their country was free again! Those living in exile for forty seven long years were able to return home without any fear of imprisonment or worse for themselves or their families.

The example of the Baltic States in 1991 inspired other nationals throughout the USSR to demand more freedom. Republics throughout the USSR now felt free to assert their national identities. On August 24 Boris Yeltsin, president of Russia, recognized Estonia's Declaration of Independence. Within a week, 30 nations had established diplomatic relations with the newly freed state. In September of 1991, Estonia became a member of the United Nations.

The nation's next order of business was to rebuild its economy and maintain a standard of living that once ranked high among former Soviet republics. They had the advantages of a well-educated population and a blend of industrial and natural resources to work with (Estonia Then and Now, p. 39).

Chapter Eleven

A Second Chance at Love

My happy marriage to Albert Sarlo, my first husband, came to an end on Christmas Day in 1976. My daughters, Susan and Esther, who are wonderful cooks, were helping me prepare our holiday meal. That morning my husband cleared the snow from our driveway.

He then headed over to the school which was a block away from our house and cleared the outdoor rink. Our son Stephen, our nephews and other local boys were then able to play hockey. Bert loved the sport and had fun playing with them.

Bert returned home exhausted and slumped into a chair--he suffered a heart attack. He never regained consciousness. Bert was only 44 years old.

Relatives rushed to our home in shock and friends always remember the day when they heard that news.

Stephen was twenty and attending Algoma University, Susan, 19 also a student at Algoma and

Esther, twelve. It was an extremely hard time for all of us. As the years passed and our grief lessoned; we were able to move on with our lives.

Stephen became a correctional officer. He married Barbara Jean Goldsmith in June 1979. They had two children. April was born on November 20, 1980 and Dustin on October 2, 1985. Susan became a French teacher and married Jim Crowe in 1983. Esther became a counselor in an alternative school and helped change the lives of many children.

After being a homemaker for twenty-one years, things changed and I went to work part time at Algoma Steel, working in various departments. Arno was employed in the Rail Mill and I sometimes worked in the scheduling office for that mill. When I had the timetables ready, it was my job to take them to the offices throughout the mill.

I would put on my hard hat, safety shoes and glasses and make the rounds. The men referred to it as 'tip-toeing through the tulips.' After we started dating, Arno told me he had seen me, walking on my circuit.

Our first official meeting was at a dinner party arranged by a mutual friend. I had been a widow for several years and had just started a new job as receptionist at a Physiotherapy Center. After meeting him, I realized I had also seen him conducting the orchestra at various theatre productions.

Arno invited me to go with him to a concert the following evening. He even offered to make dinner for me, because I did not get off work until 7:00 or later. He did not actually 'make' our meal but he ordered from Swiss Chalet. Nevertheless, it was still a treat. We dined together often, and he really prepared our meals. I was impressed!

We enjoyed going to theatre productions, concerts and other events which were going on in the art community.

I think we are drawn to someone with similar goals in life. I found Arno to be extremely gifted. The events of his earlier life honed his character and made him the man he was. I saw in him a caring person, not afraid of making a commitment. The most important characteristic for me was his love for God.

It wasn't long before he asked me to marry him. Being ever the gentleman and courtier, he got down on his knee and presented me with a lovely engagement ring. We were married on August 29, 1992.

My charming eleven year old granddaughter, April, heard the news that we were getting married and volunteered to be a bridesmaid. She looked so lovely in her pretty pink dress and was excited to have this part to play. My grandson Dustin, then a cute six-year old, was the endearing ring bearer. This was a role he thoroughly enjoyed, grinning from ear to ear as he carried the ring pillow up the aisle.

Our friend, Karen Pietkiewicz, who introduced us, was the matron of honor and one of Arno's Estonian friends Kusti Treialt, was the best man. My daughter, Esther, sang *Jesu, Joy of Man's Desiring* by J. S. Bach. Arno said that may have been the most beautiful song ever written.

We honeymooned at the delightful Lake Shore Salzburger Hof Resort on Lake Superior. We accidently locked the keys in the car and called the Automobile Association to unlock our vehicle. While waiting for CAA to arrive, we enjoyed our first meal at the resort's incredible restaurant.

We sort of tested out the swimming pool during our stay. It had been a cool summer and the pool was only heated by the sun. I put my big toe in the water. That was all the swimming for me. It was cold! Arno dove right in. I think it had something to do with his Baltic genes and being more tolerant to cold. But he wasn't in the water very long. He reluctantly admitted it was a little on the cool side.

Learning to live with someone again was also not without its challenges; eating for instance. Arno was resistant to my ideas of healthy eating. Being a man, he enjoyed eating from one main food group, fried foods. He also didn't like to waste anything when cooking. I remember one time he made chicken soup. At first he had heeded my advice on removing the skins, but only because I was there. I gave him a kiss and left for work.

Thinking it was such a waste, he put the skins in the pot and left it simmering on the stove. He then went downstairs to his study to do some work and forgot about what was cooking on the stove.

I came home from work to discover not only the kitchen walls but every room in the house covered in grimy soot! Everything had to be washed down and a new coat of paint in the kitchen put everything back to normal.

Arno's mind could be so focused on his music that it was easy for other things to escape his notice; like a pot of chicken soup bursting into flames! Events like this were not unusual in our household. Though it was NOT funny at the time—looking back we were able to laugh. Dr. Richard Swenson said, "When we can laugh at ourselves we never run out of material" (July 6, 2010). I came across a book titled: *How to Love Your Man without Losing Your Mind*. I think that book would have been extremely helpful.

We eventually came to a meeting of the minds over our diet, which Arno boasted about—having lost 25 pounds.

There were other adjustments to make as well. Arno's house was still very much Sault Opera Central and room had to be made for me and my stuff. No car had seen the inside of the garage for years.

One day when I came home from work, I saw the garage door open showing a clean interior. A big sign stating "Drive right in!" invited me to park in the garage. Arno had turned the occasion into a celebration complete with balloons and other party decorations.

After his heart attack seven years before, the doctor instructed Arno to give up at least one of his vices, smoking or drinking. Drinking was a natural part of his cultural roots, so he said good-bye to the cigarettes. Arno continued to drink but his personality changed when he drank; he had unresolved trauma and alcohol brought out the worst in him. He realized I was not happy with the situation and it was adversely affecting our relationship. Arno gave up his other vice. We did our best to make our marriage work.

Arno was also good for me. I had a deep desire to paint since I was very young and had not had the opportunity to grow in that area. He encouraged me to develop and appreciate my talents as he did for so many others. He helped me be the person I was created to be.

He gave me a Valentine one year which highlighted a side which he only showed to very few people. He wrote, "It makes such a difference in my life to have someone who understands me and cares about the things I do. That is so important to me."

Sault Opera continued to be an important part of our lives, Arno still serving as the main conductor. In 1993 he was chosen to play the lead in *Zorba the Greek*. It had been a decade since he had appeared in such a demanding on-stage role, but it was a role he couldn't resist.

Richard Howard, a professional director and adjudicator, saw in Arno qualities similar to the Zorba character—both were survivors. "They will take whatever life sends them and cope with that and it will turn them into something better," Richard said.

It was Howard's opinion that Arno's portrayal of Zorba was closer to the character created in the novel written by Nikos Kazantsakis, than Anthony Quinn's portrayal in the role, both on stage and in the movie.

Opening night the production literally exploded onto the stage depicting a human ship, sailing the ocean of life. The story is about one indomitable Greek, and his simple, uncomplicated view of living—about savoring who we are, where we are, and what we have to the fullest. To Zorba, "the only real death is the death you die every day by not living."

Arno enjoyed the role and played the part well. The company used Zorba's own philosophy to sell the show, saying, "It's a piece of life worth grabbing onto" (Waples, Sept. 13, 1993).

Richard Howard's wife, Lila Kedrova, had portrayed Madame Hortense in the movie opposite Anthony Quinn as well as the Broadway stage version of the show. She won an Oscar for best supporting actress and a Tony Award for the same role in the stage version. It was certainly a great compliment to Arno that she enthusiastically praised his performance.

In 1995 Vilma's son Peter invited us to visit him and his family in Germany to celebrate his 50th birthday. Arno's son Fred and his stepson Toomas were also invited. We were there for a little more than two weeks. What a holiday we had! Peter and his family certainly knew how to celebrate and have fun. The party lasted for two days.

While in Germany we toured castles, museums, and old churches including the church in Wittenberg where Martin Luther nailed his history-making-thesis to the door. Arno enjoyed standing in front of that door, having his picture taken. We saw many other places of historical significance as well. One was a boat tour which included seeing at a distance one of Hitler's hideouts located high on a mountain.

One evening we dined at a restaurant housed in a building built in the year 01 AD. Our menu consisted of medieval dishes. As we ate we were entertained by roaming minstrels. Our whole

visit was a wonderful, once in a lifetime experience.

Arno's Story

Chapter Twelve

An Enchanted Gala Tribute

Sault Opera wanted to honor Arno for his contribution to musical theatre and culture in Sault Ste. Marie and for his years of service. Robin Waples wrote in *The Sault Star*, September 9, 1996, "Much of the credit for Sault Opera's success is attributed to the vision, dedication and unrelenting hard work of its mentor, Arno Ambel, who recently stepped down for health reasons from his position as president, passing the baton, so to speak, to new president Norene Morrow."

Ms. Waples indicated the Gala tribute night would be held on September 13th at the Ramada Inn. "It promises to be *Some Enchanted Evening.*" The event included dinner, speeches, a slide-show waltz down Sault Opera's memory lane, musical performances and "the chance to renew old acquaintances with those who have been part of Sault Opera over the years."

The following is an excerpt from an article which appeared in the Arts Council's July/August edition of *Articulation*.

SAULT OPERA HONOURS ARNO AMBEL

"Plans are under way for an evening when the citizens of Sault Ste. Marie will have an opportunity to pay tribute to ARNO AMBEL at a banquet being given in his honor on Friday, September 13, 1996.

"In March Arno stepped down from his position as president of Sault Opera. He founded the organization in 1970 and has been its driving force for more than twenty-six years. His contribution to the cultural life of Sault Ste. Marie has been nothing short of amazing. He brought opera to a steel and hockey town and set a standard of excellence for theatre in our community.

"Due to his vision and dedication Sault Opera has mounted 56 productions. It has sponsored four Canadian Opera Company touring productions and the first four productions of the Sault Youth Theatre.

"Where did all this begin? ... in Arno's home; the heart of Sault Opera. Sets were built and stored in his garage and back yard. Costumes were made and stored in his basement, and the office was in another room. But his work did not stop there!

"Arno has spent thousands of hours in the pursuit of funding and of course, the pursuit of the best possible people for the productions both on stage and behind the scenes. His work has enriched the lives of many through the sponsoring of workshops and the acquisition of grants which has brought in professionals and provided valuable summer employment experience for students.

"While Arno will continue to be an active member of Sault Opera, the board wanted to show their appreciation through this public recognition."

The banquet was called *An Evening to Remember* and it was a night of nights–the memory of which Arno treasured. It began with a cocktail hour when people could renew old friendships and offer best wishes to Arno. The room was appropriately decorated with music notes adorning the table cloths and flowers and balloons festooned the table tops. Special music was provided by Classic Bows which consisted of Mrs. Carol O'Neill and Ms. Carmen Eisenbichler on violin and Mrs. Bernadette Merritt playing cello.

The call to dinner was announced by a town crier, Bruce Bedell. He entered the hall ringing his bell and crying "Oyez! Oyez! Oyez!" and proclaimed the following:

"SAULT OPERA'S MAJOR GENERAL"

From Eastern Europe Arno came
With culture oozing from each pore,
To North Ontario's icy climes,
To teach us shows like Pinafore.
We learned to sing in harmony,
Base, tenor and soprano.
We northern hicks, we learned so quick
We'd tackle oratorio.

But if we're sometimes out of tune,
He'd get upset so then beware,
We always knew that very soon
He'd be losing some more hair.
While listening to this maestro man
Conducting, coaching oh so slick,
And shouting G--d--- people, hey
You must learn to watch the stick!

From Opera to Broadway shows,
He's steeped in them from head to toes.
He knows the music off by heart
His reputation grows and grows.
With so much knowledge musical
Artistic and theatrical
Now he has earned the title of

Soo Opera's Major General.
T. H. 13/9/96

Mr. Terry McPhee was Master of Ceremonies and he gave the introductory remarks. He had just gotten off the plane and didn't have time to go home and change so he was in his shorts and short sleeved shirt. Arno liked what he called reverse snobbery so this made him smile; although, he was in his tux and so were many others. It was a fun filled evening with lots to make everyone laugh. Then a sumptuous dinner, carefully planned by the Ramada Inn staff, was enjoyed by everyone.

The program began with greetings and presentations from guest speakers, many who had been involved with Sault Opera with their funny or touching stories:

Mr. Herbert Johnson
Mr. Donald Roy
Mr. Rudi Becker
Mr. Steve Ballantyne

City of Sault Ste. Marie:
Mr. Udo Rauk
Mr. Charlie Swift

Arts Council of Sault Ste. Marie and District:
Mrs. Mary Capstick

Special songs of Sault Opera's past were sung. All were accompanied by Mrs. Lorraine Smith.

I Can't Give You a Good Explanation...from the *Marriage of Figaro*, sung by Ms. Norene Morrow.

Vilia...from *The Merry Widow*, sung by Jo-Ann Eagan.

The Nightingale/A Maiden Fair to See...from H.M.S. Pinafore, sung by Mr. Timothy Murphy.

Life...from *Zorba*, sung by Mrs. Teresa Caughill.

Major General's Song...from *The Pirates of Penzance*, sung by Mr. Tom Hendrie.

Sault Opera presentations were given by:

Ms. Norene Morrow

Mr. Richard and Mrs. Diane Conklin

The Corporation of the City of Sault Ste. Marie presented Arno with a plaque that evening commemorating his work (inscription on following page).

PRESENTED TO
ARNO AMBEL
FOR HIS CONTINUOUS
DEDICATION TO THE
CULTURAL DEVELOPMENT
IN SAULT STE. MARIE
AND
FOR HIS FOUNDING AND
NURTURING OF
THE SAULT OPERA SOCIETY
AND
FOR HIS CONTRIBUTION
TO THE QUALITY OF LIFE
IN OUR COMMUNITY
WITH THANKS
MAYOR STEPHEN BUTLAND AND
MEMBERS OF CITY COUNCIL

SEPTEMBER 13th 1996

Arno was then given the opportunity to express his appreciation for the accolades he received on this night of nights!

A very special scrap book was put together and presented to Arno with written greetings, anecdotes, pictures and other memorabilia. It is filled with pages and pages of letters thanking him for what his work has personally meant to them... how he brought color, verve, life and excitement to the theatre life and to their lives in general... how he was like a father to them... good and lasting memories... for helping enrich the cultural fabric of our community.

In the scrap book are two songs written about Arno by people at two different tables. They were all having fun. This one was written by four people and could be sung to the tune of *Oklahoma*.

Arno Ambel, He's Sault Opera's impresario
With his voice so deep,
His shtick so sweet
He could really bring them
To their feet.

Arno Ambel, He's the man that really
Brought them here.

The Barber and the Butcher and
The Gypsy and the Prince.

With a cast of thousands,
And a pig
We know he's the man of the day
We'd all like to say hip-hip-hooray.

We were also presented with a "carte blanche" theatre week-end in Toronto. It was fabulous! An "Executive Suite" had been reserved for us at the Royal York Hotel. What a luxurious and special time it was for us both! We were treated like royalty. Arno said it was like a second honeymoon.

Arno and I took in two operas at the Canadian Opera, Richard Strauss's *Elektra* and *Salome* as well as two musicals, *The Phantom of the Opera* at the Pantages Theatre and *Beauty and the Beast* at the Princess of Wales Theatre which were playing at the time.

Little by little Arno was letting go of the things which had been so much a part of his life. He donated the costumes that occupied the basement to the Community Theatre Center.

Norene Morrow was elected President and capably took over the load Arno had carried. She has a beautiful voice and taught voice at the Royal Conservatory of Music in the Sault.

Sadly, Norene and her husband moved away. Others stepped in and managed a couple of shows but without the driving force of Arno or Norene, the organization couldn't gather any momentum. Sault Opera mounted its last production in 1999.

Arno's son, Fred, has created a wonderful tribute to his parents by designing a website for Sault Opera. Lovingly and painstakingly, he spent hours putting it all together. It can be viewed by going to:

fredambel.brinkster.net/saultopera/

Chapter Thirteen

A Funny Thing Happened at the Opera

Anne Biggs and her family were involved in the Sault Opera during the early nineties. She shared some of her experiences with incoming Sault Opera president, Norene Morrow, in a letter in 1996.

"During our few short years in the Sault, my husband, our three children and I were members of the Sault Opera, in different capacities. It was a wonderful experience for all of us. There are so many memories, some funny, some remarkable and some touching.

"On the opening night of *Calamity Jane,* the piano stool broke and the pianist, Barbara Severin, fell into the arms of the orchestra! I'm sure it wasn't funny for Barbara—(thankfully she was not hurt)—a chair was quickly brought and Arno continued conducting the orchestra as though nothing had happened. But that little incident 'set the stage' for a series of other small 'calamities,' which were all handled with calm and finesse, by Arno. It turned out to be a rollicking success and the audience seemed to have as much fun as the company. As with so many productions, there were often mishaps, delays, or minor catastrophes, but Arno always managed to pull things together for a successful performance.

"The word 'remarkable' comes to mind when I think of the Sault Opera's production of *The Magic Flute*. I did not participate in this, but I attended the performance and found it absolutely spectacular. Not only the costumes and lighting, but the clever way in which the stand-in tenor was used after one of the leads lost his voice, made it almost impossible to tell that the actor and singer were not one and the same. Once again, what could have been a catastrophe was brilliantly handled by Arno and turned into instant success."

Barbara Severin remembered the piano stool in *Calamity Jane* as well. She wrote: "After my piano stool broke during *Calamity Jane* and I fell into the drums and cymbals during a romantic moment for Terry McPhee—he shot me in the head!"

Her son Michael played a servant in The *Gypsy Baron*. "...you had the absolutely brilliant idea of him carrying on a live pig. It seemed like a good idea in the beginning but after weeks of rehearsals what started out as cute and tiny ended up as huge, heavy and very slippery!"

It seemed Barbara learned theatre life can also be dangerous. "Who could forget playing *Cabaret* in Espanola on a six foot square stage, with me so close to the stage that one of the dancer's toes caught me on the temple and knocked me out."

In spite of the various mishaps and adventures, Barbara's experience was a positive one. "They were glorious fun-filled days of good theatre and music Arno, and Sault Ste. Marie owes you an enormous debt of gratitude."

Arno's Story

Chapter Fourteen

A Heart for God and People

God had given Arno a heart for his countrymen and his Church, the Estonian Lutheran Evangelical Church. He took his responsibilities to the congregation with as much passion as he did for theater. After their local Estonian Pastor passed away, the congregation flew in an Estonian Minister once a month to conduct services. Arno often drove to the airport to pick them up and when necessary lodged them for the night at his home.

When he could no longer play the organ, which he had done for 50 years, due to his mounting health issues, Tasha Ader volunteered. I learned to sing in Estonian, with Arno's help, of course. Arno, Tasha and I sang as a trio for these services. Arno would also prepare the bulletins and other tasks required for the services.

He visited or called elderly friends and acquaintances daily to encourage them and see if they were alright. One gentleman's eyesight was failing. Arno would go twice a week to read Estonian newspapers to him. He visited the sick, those in retirement and nursing homes as well as the hospitals.

An elderly friend in the hospital wanted to return to her home, but it had been condemned. Arno arranged for it to be repaired and made habitable. Health authorities required she needed a functioning stove as well as a bed. We were able to obtain those items and she was able to move back in. Arno also arranged for home care so she was able to continue to live there.

Another time a group of students from Fiji found themselves stranded in Sault Ste. Marie. Arno opened his home to them. There were nine in all! They called him "Dad" and formed bonds which lasted over thirty years as they kept in touch with each other. I continued to receive letters after his death and had the sad task of informing his honorary children of his passing.

Anne Biggs remembered Arno's interaction with her children who were working hard on *South Pacific*. Arno had recently stepped down as president and Anne was writing about her appreciation of having Arno and Sault Opera in their lives.

"...we have a certain memory which touched the hearts of our whole family. During the rehearsals for *South Pacific* our children worked hard, sometimes with late hours, to give their very best efforts for the show. Arno always had a kind word for them but his appreciation was really manifested the night of the cast party.

"We had not planned on allowing the children to attend, as we figured it was for adults only. When word of this reached Arno, Vilma and several other cast and production members, they all pleaded with us to allow the kids to attend, as they had 'worked so hard and were an important part of the show!'

"Because of the change of plans, we had to take the kids home to change and by the time we arrived at the restaurant, everyone had already assembled. As we entered, Arno stood up, said: 'Look who's here!' and started to applaud! Everyone in the room followed and soon the room rang with the cheers and applause of the whole company! We were all completely overwhelmed.

"I think our children were stunned and confused; they didn't understand why everyone was applauding their entry. Then Arno came forward and shook their hands and congratulated them on their performance and several others followed. It was the most sincere show of appreciation for the

efforts of three little children and is so typical of
Arno. We wanted to share this touching story with
you."

Our Wedding

My Mother, Esther, Susan, April, Dustin, B.J , Stephen, Myself, Arno, Fred, and Toomas.

Germany: Above: Arno's stepsons Toomas and Peter and son Fred. Below left: Arno and I in a marketplace. Below right: The church door in Wittenberg .

Family get together:
April, Myself, Arno,
Fred, Dustin, B.J. and
Stephen.
A Birthday Celebration
Relaxing at the beach

A Father and Son moment
Playing the Pirate
With my Mother
Peter and his wife Christa

Honoring Arno in *An Evening to Remember* Gala.
Left: Former Mayor John Rowswell presenting Arno with a plaque
Right: with town, crier Bruce Bedell

Arno's Story

Chapter Fifteen

How to Have a Life Worth Living

Arno developed and nurtured his talent for opera and was immersed in it but he knew there was more to life than musical theater. Being a complex person, searching for meaning to his life, he found solace in sacred music.

Although he had composed some music in his youth he did not have much time during his busy adult life to even think of composing and creating music. Arno, like most of us when we get older, find we have time to take a breath and do something that we have always wanted to do.

Arno's mind had been captured many years ago by a magnificent piece of music, *Panis Angelicus* (Bread of Angels). This was taken from *Sacris Solemniis,* written by St. Thomas Aquinas before the year 1274. The last two stanzas are the text for *Panis Angelicus.* It was written in Latin.

Arno spoke Estonian, English, German, Russian and some Finnish, but not Latin. He decided to go to the library for help to translate the Latin lyrics of this beautiful piece into English. He began working on it in December 1998 and after spending several months on it, he finished with the following translation which can be sung:

Panis Angelicus

(Bread of Angels)

O, bread of angels ,
Bless'd food from heaven!
Heavn'ly bread and wine,
The body and blood of our Saviour.
O, Jesus crucified! Our Saviour crucified!
Through His humble suff'ring and sacrifice
Bearing our sin and shame
He came our souls to save.
Jesus still calls us, He'll take and lead us
Safely through the darkness
On the narrow path to heaven.
O, Holy Trinity! Heavenly Trinity!
Shining bright and glorious for all eternity.
Guiding all believers to heavenly life
In eternity.

Why was this piece of music meaningful to Arno? During the war, in the thick of battle, he realized it was only God who could bring him out of it alive. Afterwards he continued to seek God for answers to the ultimate questions of life. Who am I?

Why am I here? What is my purpose? What is faith? Do I have faith? How does faith come?

The Bible says faith comes by listening to the Good News—the Good News about Jesus Christ (Romans 10:17). Arno was searching for the deeper meaning of life.

When God's people, Israel, were wandering in the wilderness for forty years, God rained down real bread, called manna, from Heaven to feed them **every morning**. This heavenly bread was vital to their existence.

Panis Angelicus is about what this Manna represents to us—Christ as "The Bread of Life." Just as the manna was vital to them, Arno learned, he needed Jesus, this true and real heavenly bread, in his life; we too need Him every day.

One of the most well-known verses in the Bible is John 3:16. *God so loved the world that he gave His one and only Son, that whoever believes in Him shall not perish but have eternal life (NIV).* This verse is saying that the purpose of God sending Jesus into the world was to save the world—to restore fellowship with Himself.

God did not send His Son into the world to condemn the world (John 3:17)—we were born condemned. The first man, Adam, was a free moral agent. When he rebelled against God and chose to disobey Him he committed high treason. It was betrayal of his God to an enemy, Satan. Satan became his god.

The LORDship of man was transferred into the hands of a spiritual outlaw, Satan (Copeland, Faith Life Challenge, 2014). Adam went against the one command God had given him— *You must not eat from the tree of the knowledge of good and evil, for when you eat of it you will surely die* (Genesis 2:17 NIV). Adam and Eve did not die immediately, or visibly, but the moment they made the decision to rebel against God, they died spiritually.

As Adam's descendants, man was born, physically alive but spiritually dead. That part of us which could know and understand God was gone. Jesus said we must have a new birth from above, in which the Spirit of God creates a new spiritual life within us. When we believe that Jesus died for our sins, that He took our sins upon Himself, paid the penalty and purchased a pardon for us, we have this new life He died to give us. He purchased the right for us to be born spiritually and have eternal life.

The Creator loved us so much that He **gave** His one and only Son. Jesus had to leave Heaven,

His eternal residence, and took on human life. The obstacles were too great for man to remove them apart from God coming to the rescue. A complete change of attitude regarding sin and God was needed.

Jesus loved us and **gave** His life for us. The greatest sin we can commit is the rejection of Jesus as our Lord and Savior—that is the one unpardonable sin (John 16:9). The very fact that God gave Jesus—His best—for us, tells us that God wants the very best for our life.

This is God's dream for man. It is a choice, a decision, to receive Jesus as our Lord and Savior. This great Hymn, *Panis Angelicus*, tells us of these wonderful truths. Its words lead to the table of Life, upon which God has prepared a feast for us of the Bread of Angels—His own beloved Son—our Bread from Heaven.

If we eat of this Bread, we can walk forever in the fullness of His love, and our song will release its very joy, gladness and thanksgiving throughout creation!

Arno's Story

Chapter Sixteen

How to Fulfill Life's Purpose

Arno particularly appreciated the poetry of Peeter Sink, a well-known Estonian pastor and poet. Most of the pieces of music Arno wrote were inspired by Sink's verse. Two of his books are in my library.

Sink also lived through the war. Based on his experiences learning to trust and depend upon the Lord, his poetry is filled with depth and feeling. He writes about the things that are really important—the things that give meaning and purpose to life. *And this is the way to have eternal life—by knowing you, the only true God, and Jesus Christ, the one you sent to earth!* (John 17:3 TLB). That is what is important—knowing our Father God, His love, His thoughts, His ways, His attitudes and His standards for living, through a personal intimate relationship. War has a way of distinguishing between the things that matter and things that don't.

Because of Arno's own involvement in the war, he identified with the thoughts and feelings

Peeter so ably expressed. He too experienced the reality of God's presence with him in the battle.

But where Arno had escaped the communist rule of the Soviet Union, Sink had remained in Estonia, persecuted by the rulers of the Soviet-dominated country.

The inspiration for Arno's music would often come to him in the middle of the night—he would get up and compose. Often he wrote in the two books, along with a notation of the date and time the inspiration came to him. Away from the piano, he simply heard the music in his soul and put it down on paper.

A fun loving person, he chose productions for the theatre which would lift your spirits and make you laugh, but the thoughts filling his mind when he created music were all of a spiritual nature.

By the Altar was one of Sink's pieces of poetry for which Arno composed music. Although still involved in theatre, this piece had a special significance for him. Things were changing in his life. In an interview, Norene Morrow said: "Arno avoids words such as 'retired.' Sault Opera is his child to whom he gave birth, nurtured, and watched grow up. He will continue working for Sault Opera as long as it is humanly possible" (Waples, 1996).

It is hard to let go of something that has been so important in your life—but Arno had not let go of his music!

Two months after he wrote the music for *By the Altar* he translated it from Estonian into English. The Zion Evangelical Lutheran Church we attended asked me to sing it. It has also been sung in other Churches across Canada and the United States. There is a recording of this song being sung by an opera singer, Dr. Caroline Helton, at a Palm Sunday Estonian service in Detroit, Michigan in 2002. She sang it so beautifully in Estonian.

By The Altar

I don't know, I don't know–
How I can give myself to serve You.
Just take me as I stand before You now.

I don't know, I don't know–
What offering I have to bring You.
I'll give You everything I've called my own.

Yes I know, Yes, I know–
I cannot find my own direction
Without the helping hand You offer me.

I don't know, even how–
To save my life here any longer.
My skills, my strength, my life are Yours alone.

It's Your will, It's Your will–
The sunset of my life approaches.
I don't want to waste the hours left to me!

Here I am, Here I am!–

Peeter Sink was searching for the goal of personal spiritual acquaintance. His confidence was in God—his tower of strength. He had a passionate yearning for divine reality.

This was an especially difficult quest because the Crusaders, who brought the story of Jesus to Estonia, took their land from them and made them slaves. Their conduct was shocking; they were cruel and greedy and outraged the Estonians.

The Crusaders brought a totally wrong concept of God; God is love. Jesus came to set the captives free, to loose people from Satan's deception and bring them to a spacious place of joy, freedom, authenticity, and transparency.

Satan wants to keep people bound. It is the devil who came to steal, kill and destroy. The Bible describes Satan in John 8:44 as the father of lies—using pretension and deception—no truth is in him. This was a dark chapter in Estonia's history. It left the Estonian people with a legacy of unresolved understanding of the true character of God and it has had a lasting and damaging impact on their culture. A study in 2005 indicated only 16% of Estonians expressed a belief in God, the lowest in the countries examined (Estonia, N.D.).

It has made it difficult for people to find God. But God has promised; *you will seek me and find me when you seek me with all your heart* (Jeremiah 29:13 NIV). Peeter Sink found Him and realized the privilege of knowing and loving God is unfathomable. He poured out his life on God's altar—yielded his life to theLordship of Jesus Christ, and made every effort to fulfill God's calling in his life—to know Him, to love Him, to serve Him.

Arno too, in his pursuit of God, had these lies to confront. He also wanted more than just a form of the Christian life. Ultimately Arno found Him and what God was calling him to do.

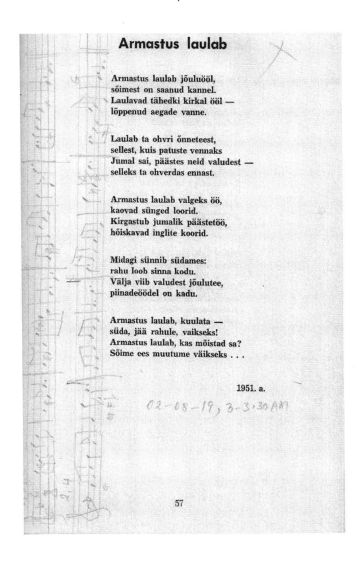

Armastus laulab

Armastus laulab jõuluööl,
sõimest on saanud kannel.
Laulavad tähedki kirkal ööl —
lõppenud aegade vanne.

Laulab ta ohvri õnneteest,
sellest, kuis patuste vennaks
Jumal sai, päästes neid valudest —
selleks ta ohverdas ennast.

Armastus laulab valgeks öö,
kaovad sünged loorid.
Kirgastub jumalik päästetöö,
hõiskavad inglite koorid.

Midagi sünnib südames:
rahu loob sinna kodu.
Välja viib valudest jõulutee,
piinadeöödel on kadu.

Armastus laulab, kuulata —
süda, jää rahule, vaikseks!
Armastus laulab, kas mõistad sa?
Sõime ees muutume väikseks . . .

1951. a.

57

Arno's musical notations for one of Peeter Sink's poems written in the margin. *Rännutee Laulud* , Toronto, 1962

151

Arno's Story

Chapter Seventeen

We at our Best are Flawed Human Beings

Arno was quite a guy but he wasn't a perfect man. Everyone who knew him knew that. "If we expect to get all the way through life without embarrassing ourselves, without playing the fool, without needing the unmerited favor of God...well, it's just not going to happen. We are too human—all of us" (Burnham, 2006). We are all a work in progress.

In the war he had been subjected to evil that lurks in man. He experienced destruction, pain, suffering, racism, crying and death; the depths to which man can sink—the depravity of the human heart. Anger festered in him. Nothing in life prepared him to handle such anger. He learned people who had not gone through this experience did not have the frame of reference to understand such emotional havoc.

How did Arno deal with these issues? They did not disappear over-night—it's a journey. In Arno's case it was a long journey. He needed a power greater than his own. The Apostle Paul struggled with this problem and found that deliverance comes only through Jesus Christ.

I see another law at work in the members of my body, waging war against the law of my mind and making me a prisoner of the law of sin at work within my members. What a wretched man I am! Who will rescue me from this body of death? Thanks be to God—through Jesus Christ our Lord! (Romans 7:23-25 NIV).

He is our source. It is Christ living in us that gives us the wisdom and strength to be who God created us to be. *The mystery that has been kept hidden for ages and generations, but is now disclosed to the saints. To them God has chosen to make known among the Gentiles the glorious riches of this mystery, which is Christ in you, the hope of glory* (Colossians 1: 26-27 NIV).

It is Jesus who enables us to have the abundant life He died to give us; not just getting us into heaven but getting us into a better life. It is a life entirely new. 100 years ago A. B. Simpson wrote about this truth and how it completely changed his life. "*And the life I now live in the flesh, I live,*" not by faith in the Son of God, but "*by the faith of the Son of God*" (Galatians 2:20 KJV)

(Simpson, p. 14). The energy of His faith enables us to do His will—it is a fountain of life for all we need. This is a life that only Christ can give us.

Man looks on the outward appearance but God looks at the heart—at the inner man. It is the heart that needs to be transformed.

Nelson Mandela, known as South Africa's greatest son, taught the world it's possible to transform anger into hope (Stories, 2013, December 8)—he was able to forgive. Jesus wants us to be free from our prison—this requires forgiveness.

Johnny Cash battled addictions, depression and many troubles. He sang a song, written by Billy Shaver: *I'm just an old chunk of coal, now Lord But I'm gonna be a diamond some-day.* Johnny had put his life into God's loving hands; that is how Arno too was set free. He handed over these perplexing and difficult matters he struggled with to God.

Arno also came to understand God could use the darkest moments in his life to his benefit. His life was not shattered, but strengthened by what he experienced. As a result all of these things that challenged his identity and dignity, freedom and rights became a dominant thought permeating every aspect of his life.

Arno's heart was failing. It had gotten to the point where he was becoming bed ridden. He had a pacemaker implanted in 2000. It worked wonderfully for him. He thanked God for the technology available today. It gave him another four years--mostly good.

That year Arno resumed working on another one of Sink's poems. It was *Jesus is Born,* one that had occupied his mind and heart at the time when his parents arrived in Canada. The music begins: *Jesus is born, O take heart and be happy!*

This poem had special meaning to him because he was overjoyed to be able to bring his parents here after their 19 years of separation—during most of which no contact with them was allowed. That is a long time! *Kristus on tulnud (Jesus is Born!)* was performed on December 19, 2003 at Vana-Andrese Kotukus (St. Andrews Church) in Toronto, Ontario. Arno was pleased his work was being acknowledged.

An Estonian Lutheran Pastor, Kirsti Kimmel, arranged for Arno's compositions to be displayed in a museum in Tallinn. His biography was included with the sheet music. Reverend Kimmel has been responsible for Arno's compositions being sung at various Estonian Lutheran Churches throughout Canada and the U.S.

Arno's Story

Chapter Eighteen

Walking Down Memory Lane

Many summer days we drove to Tower Lake, about half an hour drive from the Sault. It is an idyllic, peaceful spot. Usually alone there, we basked in the sunshine. Arno loved these excursions. For several years his knees had been giving him trouble. He started using a walker to help him get around. He enjoyed swimming and these outings gave him the opportunity to benefit from the exercise he could do easily, proficiently, and it was therapeutic.

Being a nature lover, these outings fed his soul. We often packed a picnic lunch to enjoy in this setting. Two loons were in residence on the lake. It thrilled us at the end of the day to see them circling twice to rise above the trees and fly safely and elegantly away. Their departure was the signal that it was time for us to go home too.

Sometimes on a week end our family would join us. About two years before Arno passed away, the family was together when he decided to swim all the way around the small lake. It was a scary feat, but he accomplished this goal with the same determination he applied to all his activities.

Arno's son and my two daughters lived out of town. They would sometimes come and spent the holidays with us and my son's family here in the Sault. Time spent together with our families was important and deeply meaningful to us.

We still enjoyed and attended the many concerts and theatre production, not only in our city, but across the Ste. Mary's River in Michigan.

The Estonians celebrated their Independence Day, St. John's Day and other Estonian holidays at a lodge they owned in Goulais River.

Arno never missed celebrating any of these events. As the people got older they sold the lodge but they continued to meet for these holidays at a restaurant.

Arno often spoke at these gatherings giving a short talk about Estonian traditions or holidays. He would also lead the singing of the Estonian national anthem and other songs in the Estonian language. We then shared a wonderful meal in this common bond. These were good times— important times to him—with people who shared cultural roots and who he deeply respected and cared for.

February 23, 2014, was the 96th anniversary of their Independence Day and, although they are fewer in number, and are getting older, they are still commemorating it.

A program on television caught my attention one day called "The Musical Brain" (April 7, 2011). It was especially interesting to me because I knew for a certainty that Arno had a musical brain. The narrator on the program said music speaks the language of the spirit and heart. Shortly after I had watched the program I was visiting an Estonian lady, to whom I had loaned one of Arno's books of poetry by Peeter Sink.

She was finished with it and I brought it home with me. As I leafed through it later that evening I was amazed with what Arno had written, the musical scores to a number of the poems, and a record of the dates he composed them. I had tears in my eyes as I ran my fingers over Arno's handwriting in the margins of this book and the scraps of paper serving as bookmarks. It was the first time I had seen these notes. There was page after page in his neat script; music for the words speaking to his heart.

With his health continuing to decline in 2002, he immersed himself in composing music.

On one page in Sink's book he noted: August 17th at 8:00 a.m. to 10:00 a.m. he composed one piece of music. On August 18th the next day, he composed three pieces between four and six a.m. The day after that, he composed another three pieces in the early hours of the morning. After looking through the first book of Sink's poems I thought I would look in his other book and found many more musical scores Arno had written to his words. One book contains 314 poems and the other 92.

While visiting my Estonian friends Helgi and Erich, Helgi translated some of these poems for me. It touched me to know what Arno's thoughts were during his intense, concentrated effort.

One of the poems was titled, *In the Evening*. The words translated into English were:

Is my work done?
Is my labor noticed?
Can I go home?
I would like to do a lot before the sun goes down.
I plant seeds here and there.

Another poem was titled *So Sure*:

It is so sure to be in His hands,
He who has created Heaven and Earth.
He carries me, takes care of me so I cannot fall,

And never leaves me alone.

It is so good to be in His hands.
That is where there is peace and rest for me.
Let storms come, winds and the sea,
They in everything obey His will.
In His hands is my strength and victories,
And that is enough for my soul.

The translation of *Take Me to You*:

Take me Lord.
I reach my hand toward you.
I can't see one step in front of me.
But because you take me,
I will never go wrong.
Every step of the road becomes schooling for me.
I am not frightened by storms or the noise of war.
My tongue will sing about your miracles of love.
Take Me to You.
Peeter Sink, Taeva vari, (*The Sky Shadow*) "translated by Helgi Männiste."

Both Helgi and her husband liked the poetry. They made the observation Arno seemed to know as he was composing this music, his time was short.

Arno's Story

Chapter Nineteen

Sacred Songs of Love and Joy

Two poems for which Arno wrote the music were about Christmas. I encouraged Arno to translate more of his work into English so it could be sung and understood here in Canada. He wanted to translate *Love* Sings, this lovely Sacred Song for us to perform in 2002 as a quartet for the Christmas Eve service at the Zion Lutheran Evangelical Church.

Not feeling well or up to the task at that time—he translated the meaning of the words to my daughter, Esther, who lives in Vancouver, British Columbia. She had the skill to ably make them fit the music. Thankfully Arno was well enough to join Noel Beer, Ann Scott and myself to sing for that special service. The message of Christmas is an incredible love story! We are loved!

We celebrate Christmas with giving because Jesus was the greatest gift that compassion has ever given. "They shall call His Name Emmanuel," which means, God at last, is with us.

Love Sings
(This Christmas Night)
Armastus Laulab Jõuluööl

Love sings this Christmas night,
The manger becomes a lyre.
Even the Stars sing tonight,
The curse's power has ended.

Love sings a song of truth,
God becomes one of us.
To save us from all misery,
He gives Himself an offering

Love sings night into day,
Veils of darkness vanish.
Salvation radiates promise,
Choirs of angels are singing.

Love sings of something new,
Hearts are a home for peace.
The soul of Christmas soothes our pain,
Empty nights are vanquished.

Love is singing, listen!
Be serene and quiet,
Love is singing, understand?
At manger's foot we become small,
So small.

Original (Estonian) Text by Peeter Sink, 1951
English Translation by Esther Sarlo, 2002
Music by Arno Ambel, 2002

When the angel of The Lord came to announce Jesus' birth it was one of the most earth-shaking events of all time! His voice shook the earth! The fields vibrated with his words as he delivered the message of Almighty God: *I bring you good news of great joy that will be for all the people* (Luke 2:10 NIV).

The Savior—the Deliverer the Jews had hoped and prayed for so long—had finally been born! The angel was also telling them Jesus had come to bring the joy of the Lord, not only to the Jews, but to all people. *Suddenly there was with the angel a multitude of heavenly host praising God, and saying Glory to God in the highest, and on earth peace, good will toward men!* (Matthew 1:23 KJV) (Copeland, The Blessing of the Lord, p.p. 153-155, 2011).

Jesus Is Born

(Kristus On Tulnud)

Jesus is born, O give thanks and be happy!
Angels in heaven proclaim the good news.
The baby you'll find in Bethlehem's manger,
The living God's Son is in Bethlehem!

Jesus is born, O give thanks and be happy!
Praise and thanksgiving our lips shall proclaim,
Praise and thanksgiving our lips shall proclaim.

Jesus is born, He's that child in the manger.
He's Heavenly King yet brother to you!
He has brought peace, and solace from troubles.
Peace He has brought, and salvation, too.

Christ has arrived, and this child in the manger,
Forgives all our sins and brings blessings untold,
Forgives all our sins and brings blessings untold.

Christ has arrived, and the heavens are open.
Christmas Night's splendour brightens our eyes.
We'll go on our Mission to those who are waiting
To hear the promised One has been born.

Christ has arrived, and the heavens are open.

Love can unite us so there can be peace,
Love can unite us so there can be peace.

Christ is our Saviour! Christ is our Saviour!
Rejoice, O rejoice!

Lyrics: Original version in Estonian language by an unknown author.
Translation to English language: Arno and Janis Ambel, August 2004.
Music and S.A.T.B. Setting: Arno Ambel, December 1964, November 2000 and August 2004.

Real Joy is another lovely poem, written by Peeter Sink, for which Arno composed music. When he translated poetry from Estonian to English he liked to have my input—he included my name on his sheet music.

Joy

Rõõm

Joy is to be a child of God going forward.
Though trials will come,
We're under His care.
Joy is to see His glory and wonders,
To feel His love and care—
Through all my days.

Arno's Story

Joy is to know my heavenly Father
Is always near me,
He'll never leave me, He gives me all I need.
God sees my ways and knows my deeds,
Still He shields me from harm
Through the trials of life.

Joy is to draw near Him
When burdened with troubles,
He gives me comfort in my distress.
Joy is to tell Him my worries,
And to marvel how everything's
Put in order again.

When I feel worthless
And my heart is breaking,
He won't turn me away
When I ask for His aid.
He offers His help to all who are hurting,
His love and mercy are boundless to all.

Lyrics: Peeter Sink,

English Translation: Arno and Janis Ambel

Tune: Arno Ambel, July 10, 2002

Arno had been seeking for joy which would bring a deep lasting inner peace. He came to understand the words, the theory, the ideas and doctrine about Christ in our mind are not enough but merely the outward expressions and symbols of the spiritual reality. He wanted to experience this joy; live a joy filled life. He sought for glimpses of God's heart, His nature, and His love.

This starts on the inside. He knew happiness was not enough—it is about the good things that happen to us but they can go in a flash. He had experienced success in his area of expertise, music. But the joy, the peace, the true confidence he was seeking the world could not give him. It is rooted in God—it can't be taken from us—it fills the deep, empty place in our heart.

God created us with a cavernous need that we would seek to fill until we have found Him. It is His presence that gives us hope and joy. Real joy is ours when we have the person of Jesus Christ Himself living in us. That is the secret, *the revelation of the mystery hidden for long ages past, but now revealed and made known* (Romans 16:25-26 NIV).

Christ living in us is the only way we are enabled to live the life we were created to live. Arno chose to set his gaze on our miracle-working God—

what we focus on, that is where our faith and trust will go.

Chapter Twenty

Arno Perseveres

Arno had been improving health-wise. In May 2003 a serious and life-threatening condition arising from an insufficient blood supply in a toe developed gangrene. The doctors wanted to amputate his foot. Because there was a blockage of blood flow high on the leg, Arno knew, in all probability, he would end up losing more than just his foot. The wound from the amputation would not likely heal, and the rest of his leg would then have to be removed.

Consulting with his doctors, he asked if there was anything else they could do. They decided to perform bypass surgery on his leg. Arno and I were grateful for the wonderful, caring doctors God provided in this hour. Because of his heart condition, regular anesthetic was out of the question. He endured this operation with a local one. Knowing he might not survive the surgery, it was very courageous of Arno to go through with it. How thankful we were that he did survive it—God had helped him over another, difficult hurdle.

Arno often joked his way through difficult times. This was no exception. He brought a smile to the anesthetist face with the courageous humor he maintained through his four hour ordeal.

While Arno was in the hospital, I moved from our house to an apartment. We had a lovely split level home, but climbing the stairs would have been nearly impossible for Arno. The house sold quickly and we settled into apartment living.

The Lord directed us to an apartment on the ninth floor of a clean, secure building with, of course, an elevator. The management kindly gave us a convenient parking spot close to the back door. This proved a great advantage when Arno was able to go out again. The large windows sweeping from the ceiling almost to the floor were another blessing, letting in the light which brightened our spirits. It was hard for Arno to move from our lovely house, but he was very thankful for this spacious, sunlit apartment.

After leaving the hospital, Arno had a nurse come every day. At first it was to dress the wound from the by-pass surgery on his leg as well as his toe. When the leg wound healed they continued to come for many months to dress the wound in his toe. He had several subsequent bouts of serious infection in his toe, but we were able to gain some insight into how to deal with these, so he did not have a reoccurrence of the infections.

Then I learned how to dress the wound so it was not necessary for the nurses to come anymore. While Arno was going through all this, he still maintained a buoyant outlook—he was not one to be discouraged or depressed. The gangrene never completely healed but it did continue to decrease in size.

He did gain healing and strength. He was so glad to be able to get 'out and about' again, and we were able to get back to doing the things we had so much previously enjoyed.

Arno was able to be a part of *Judas Maccabeus*, a special performance with massed choir and orchestra, conducted by Paul Dingle. G. F. Handel's Oratorio took place at Central United Church on Saturday, March 6, 2004.

There were 42 in the choir. It really was a special performance. I was able to sing with the choir also. Arno's pacemaker needed adjusting at that time and it was difficult for him but as always he persevered and was able to do it and enjoyed himself. He did get help with his pacemaker and we were glad of that

Arno's love of music did not wane during the last months and weeks of his life, it only intensified. On a Sunday about seven weeks before his passing we sang a duet at the Zion Evangelical Lutheran Church where we attended. It was a Sacred Song titled *Come to Me*, which was based on the Gospel of Matthew 11:28-30.

The piano accompaniment for this beautiful piece of music is taken from the First Movement of the *Moonlight* Sonata by Ludwig van Beethoven. The congregation applauded Arno's efforts, but he gestured that it was to God's glory.

COME TO ME

Come to me, Come to me,
All ye that need rest.
Take my yoke, take my yoke
Upon you and learn of Me.
All ye that labor, all ye that are heavy laden:
I will give you rest.
I am meek, I am meek,
I am lowly, lowly in heart.
For I am meek, meek in heart.

Come to me, Come to me
All ye that need rest.
Come to me, Come to me

To find rest unto your souls.
My yoke is easy, my burden light,
My yoke is easy and my burden is light, is light.
O, come to me, all ye, to find rest,
Come to me.
Amen

Beethoven, Ludwig van (adapted by Alexander Aslanoff). *Come to Me*, Op. 27, No. 2. Solo voice with Piano, Harp or Organ accompaniment. Baritone and Alto voices added by Arno Ambel July 2 and August 6, 2002.

This passage of scripture, taken from The Message Bible reads as follows: *Are you tired? Worn out? Burned out on religion? Come to me. Get away with me and you'll recover your life. I'll show you how to take a real rest. Walk with me and work with me—watch how I do it. Learn the unforced rhythms of grace. I won't lay anything heavy or ill-fitting on you. Keep Company with me and you'll learn to live freely and lightly* (Matt 11:28-30 MSG).

People ask the question, "What does it mean to be at rest? In the midst of our hectic, on-the-go pace of life, is real rest even possible?" These verses are for those whose wearisome efforts to achieve spiritual rest have not eased the burden of man-made obligations.

It is for those who are conscious of need. Spiritual awareness of Christ is not arrived at through intellect or common sense. It is for those who recognize their spiritual helplessness that are able to receive Christ's teaching.

In this difficult time of Arno's life he needed to find rest for his soul. By nature we have a toiling mentality. We try to do things in our own strength. That is not the life God wants for us. He wants us to live in peace and at rest. Arno learned in some measure to do what God wants us to do—He wants us to roll all our cares, in every area of our life, over on Him—to have a relationship with Him—to know Him. God wants to bless us beyond our wildest dreams—when we stop trying to earn His blessing.

Another piece of music Arno had just finished arranging for us to sing as a duet was Handel's *I Know That My Redeemer Liveth*. Sadly, he did not live long enough for us to sing this timeless hymn.

I Know that my Redeemer Liveth

I know that my redeemer liveth,
And that He shall stand at the latter day,
Upon the earth.
And though worms destroy this body,
Yet in my flesh shall I see God.

I know that my redeemer liveth.
For now is Christ risen from the dead,
The first fruits of them that sleep.

These words were spoken by the ancient Biblical Patriarch Job in the abyss of despair. On top of the calamity which had befallen him he was being attacked and accused in the harshest way possible by his so called friends.

Yet in the face of all of this, Job cried aloud, "I KNOW that my Redeemer lives." In spite of everything, Job knew God would 'come through' for him; that He would rescue, deliver, and set him free from it all.

Job learned all that from looking at nature. *Since earliest times men have seen the earth and sky and all God made, and have known of His existence and great eternal power* (Romans 1:20 TLB). Psalm 19:1-6 also says: *The heavens are telling the glory of God; they are a marvelous display of his craftsmanship. Day and night they keep on telling about God. Without a sound or word, silent in the skies, their message reaches out to all the world.* (TLB)

In Creation's very continuance, Job saw hope for himself, at the hands of this loving, life-giving God. Surely, if He would so faithfully sustain the sky, and the sea; the meadows and the trees—even the tiny sparrow, He would not leave him—without His tender help. Not only is He the great Creator, but He is also a caring and loving God.

Today, we have God's Word that tells us God is love as well as creation. Arno went through a really dark valley when he was in the war and in numerous other situations. Like Job he was set free by knowing that his Redeemer lives. Jesus rose from the dead—Jesus *lives.* This truth began the healing process—knowing he was loved by the great Creator released Arno from the chains that bound him—showing him the path to life, peace and joy. *You have made known to me the path of life; you will fill me with joy in your presence* (Psalm 16:11 NIV).

The truths expressed in the sacred songs Arno loved, and the poetry to which he composed

music, helped him to find peace and gave the healing he so desperately needed for the battle that
raged in his heart—that almost destroyed him.
God wants to bring us healing, but more than anything, He wants us to *know* our Healer. He wants
to give us resurrection life, but more than that, He
wants us to *know* the Resurrection and the Life
(Moore, 2009). It is not just having Him meet our
needs—He wants us to have an intimate relationship with Him. Jesus prayed, *This is eternal life:
that they may know you, and Jesus Christ whom
you have sent* (John 17:3 NIV).

Arno's Story

Chapter Twenty-One

A Life Remembered

We had been in our apartment for about 16 months. It was August 27th. Arno had just finished doing some online banking when I heard him fall. I rushed to the bedroom to find him unconscious. He had stopped breathing!

I called 911 and started artificial respiration. By the time the paramedics arrived Arno had started breathing again. They took over and quickly transported him to the hospital. The staff was wonderful and gave him the best care possible.

Our family and a few close friends held vigil with me in his room. My granddaughter, April, smuggled in her tiny dog which she carried around in her purse. I wondered if Tequila's presence would cause a problem. The nurses took the dog around to every patient in Intensive Care, who were each delighted with the diversion.

Sadly, my dear husband never regained consciousness. On August 30, 2004, I was at Arno's bedside. I became aware that he had stopped breathing. He had lived 77 years—all of them to the full.

Arno's physician Doctor Maloney happened to be in the hospital at that moment. He came into Arno's room. He told me how he enjoyed Arno's humor when he came to the office and how it brightened his day. It was comforting to hear these kind words.

The celebration of Arno's life was in Estonian and English. It took place at the Zion Lutheran Evangelical Church. The building was filled to capacity that day. Many people came to offer their sympathy and to show their respect for Arno. The Estonian Lutheran Archbishop, Udo Petersoo, flew in from Toronto to officiate at Arno's funeral.

Udo Rauk Director of Operations and Manager of Education and Outreach for the Ontario Association of Chiefs of Police (OACP), gave the eulogy and smiled as he said that Arno would now be directing a choir in heaven. Arno and I had sung in the Zion choir for a number of years. That day the choir under the direction of Karen Kettles sang hauntingly *Peace be with you.*

My young great-niece Christine Aceti, sang some of Mozart's music; because the composer had been Arno's favorite. She sang from her heart and with such feeling. The Sault Star reported her "voice floated like that of an angel across the hushed congregation."

Paul Dingle, an excellent pianist and music teacher at Algoma Conservatory, played a splendid piano arrangement during the service. He later expressed his gratitude for Arno who had paved the way for himself and others, to be where they are today.

Many people spoke to me about the influence Arno had in their lives. One man said that being in the plays helped him to keep his sanity during a period in his life when he was really struggling. He was an excellent actor and continued to act when he moved away from the Sault.

Someone else told me Arno cast him for a part when he knew nothing about music or acting and worked with him. He became an exceptionally good actor and played the lead role in many productions.

A man shared Arno knew just what to do and how to do it. I agreed with him. I had seen Arno's deftness more than once in action. I remember hearing Arno show a young girl how to do operatic runs and she is now winning prestigious awards in many countries as an opera singer and playing the lead role in operas.

In Memoriam, Karin Seidemann wrote, in the Art's Council Magazine, "On September 2, 2004, Sault Ste. Marie said farewell to a man who helped shape the cultural landscape of our city: Arno Ambel. He was a man with a vision who, like so many others in this city, earned a living by working at Algoma Steel. But his passion was music. Arno was a musical pioneer, a man who changed the musical scene of Sault Ste. Marie" (Seidemann, 2004).

Arno had a unique ability to inspire and motivate people. He had a vision of what could be accomplished with music and lived to see it fulfilled. His life encourages us also to have a vision and a hope, whether it is for peace, health, happiness, or something far beyond even that and believe that it will happen.

Arno looked at what the end would be, and did not lose heart through the time and obstacles that came in reaching his goals. He achieved his dream and influenced others by the good of it. It was God who gave him this gift and enabled him to realize his vision.

It was extremely important for Arno that what he did in the field of music might touch the hearts and minds of people. Many pieces of music he loved are iconic, powerful pieces. When beautiful music is attached to a prayer, it affects us in a personal way.

The older we get these things become all the more meaningful. Historian David McCullough once said, "Take away American music from the American story and you take away a good part of the soul of the story. It's impossible to imagine life in America without it" (McCullough, 2013, November 1).

Arno gave people the opportunity to be involved in something that would not have been possible had it not been for his vision and knowledge.

Arno's Story

Chapter Twenty-Two

A Legacy Remains

Bill Slingsby, Past President of the Arts Council of Sault Ste. Marie and District praised Arno's ability to encourage area residents to appreciate their gifts. "He had a way of making sure people acknowledged their own abilities, which is a significant thing." "Arno recognized that the people of Sault Ste. Marie were as talented as or even more talented than some of the professional artists," he said (Kelly, 2004).

Arno had a dream, a vision for his life and for the people of his culture. He lived his life with purpose and passion. I do not know of anyone who set about to pursue their vision as determinedly as he. All the dark, troublesome times Arno experienced during the war, the loneliness and hardship he encountered in coming to a new country...all these struggles were the very things which enabled him to do what he did in this community, both in music and in showing compassion.

Ultimately he acknowledged his dependence upon Jesus Christ as the source of his strength. He recognized the gifts he was given and used them to serve others and bring glory to God.

Arno's legacy is not completely wrapped up in the work he did with Sault Opera, conducting choirs, or even in his compositions. His greatest legacy is in those lives he touched. As I reread the many letters he received from various people I think this legacy is best expressed in their words.

"Having the chance to witness the affection and respect in which you are held makes it possible to understand the decades of dedicated service. Well done." (Rev. Allan Reed)

"You have brought color, verve, life and excitement to the Sault's theatre life and to all of our lives in general." (Sharon Sproule)

"Thanks for the fun! Soo Opera is a bright spot in Sault culture! You are worth your weight in gold!" (Shane Halpin)

"Thanks for giving me my beginnings on stage, a wonderful part of my life. You were always as a father to me and encouraged me always." (Jo-Ann (Morgan) Egan)

"Thanks for giving me the chance to 'climb over rocky-mountains'—it changed my life and that of my students! I'll always be 'Maria, meine Kleine.'" (Maria Burgess)

"Armanda degli Abbati would be oh so proud. Thank you for the years of dedication and commitment you have given. Bless you especially for encouraging and believing in me." (Carrie Apostle)

"Your influence in producing such talent in the Sault will be remembered for a long time." (David Cook)

"You Arno have contributed to peace and the wellbeing of everyone who has experienced your music." (Joan Foster)

"All I can think about is the good times we had while tromping through the hearts and flowers." (Steve Ballantine)

"They were glorious fun-filled days of good theatre and music Arno, and Sault Ste. Marie owes you an enormous debt of gratitude." (Barbara Saylor-Severin)

"I love you Arno." (Lila Kedrova)

"God bless you Arno and much love." (Richard Howard)

"The names Sault Opera Society and Arno Ambel have become nearly synonymous in Sault

Ste. Marie. Your love of music combined with your many years of dedicated hard work, have been a rich cultural blessing to our whole community." (Rev. James Garey)

Mr. Opera!

A Beautiful Voice

A beautiful voice
And a brave heart stood still.
Their mission accomplished,
It was God's will.
He filled our lives with music and song.
With enormous talent
And passion so strong,
He succeeded in what
No one believed he could do.
To bring opera and operetta
To a steel town like the Soo.
When his health overwhelmed him
And changed his life,
He still found strength
In his faith and in his wife.
Arno gave all he had to give,
And through his music he will live.

(Poem by Karin Von Althen)

Sault Opera: Zorba 1993 2004.10 Scrapbook 55 Courtesy of Sault Ste. Marie Public Library (ssmpl.ca)

Works Cited

Armanda degli Abbati-Campodonico. (N.D.). Retrieved from http://translate.google.ca/translate?hl=en&sl=et&u=http://et.wikipedia.org/wiki/Armanda_degli_Abbati-Campodonico&prev=/search%3Fq%3Darmanda%2Bdegli%2Babbati%26client%3Dfirefox-a%26hs%3DX65%26rls%3Dorg.mozilla:en-US:official: http://translate.google.ca/translate?hl=en&sl=et&u=http://et.wikipedia.org/wiki/Armanda_degli_Abbati-Campodonico&prev=/search%3Fq%3Darmanda%2Bdegli%2Babbati%26client%3Dfirefox-a%26hs%3DX65%26rls%3Dorg.mozilla:en-US:official

Burnham, G. (2006). *To Fly Again. p. 90.* Carol Stream, Illinois: Tyndale House Publishers, Inc.

Campbell, D. (1997). *The Mozart Effect.* New York, N.Y.: Avon Books.

Canfield, J. (n.d.). *The Secret Law of Attraction.*

Chambers, O. (n.d.).

Churchill, W. S. (n.d.). *The Grand Alliance.*

Copeland, K. (2011). *The Blessing of the Lord, p.p. 153-155.* Fort Worth, TX: Kenneth Copeland Publications.

Copeland, K. (2014). Faith Life Challenge. *Faith Life e-institute.* Langly BC: Kenneth Copeland Ministries.

Curran, J. (June 29, 1966). Sault Ste. Marie, ON: Sault Star.

Department, G. (1992). *Estonia Then and Now.* Minneapolis, Minn.: Lerner Publications Company.

Estonia. (N.D.). Retrieved from Wikipedia.org: http://en.wikipedia.org/wiki/Estonia#Religion

Estonia Then and Now. (1992). Minneapolis, Minn.: Lerner Publications Company, Geography Dept.

Estonia Then and Now, p. 37. (1992). Minneapolis, Minn.: Lerner Publications Company, Geography Department.

Estonia Then and Now, p. 39. (1992). Minneapolis, Minn.: Lerner Publications Company, Geography Dept.

German, G. (1979). "*Merelinn Tallinn.* Tallinn , Estonia": Kirjastus, Esti Raamat.

German, G. (n.d.). *Merelinn Tallinn.*

(July 6, 1962). Sault Ste. Marie, ON: Sault Star.

(July 6, 2010).

Kelly, B. (2004, September 2). Opera Society's Ambel shared his love of music with the Sault. *The Sault Star.*

Männiste, H. (2008). *The Children's Book, p. 323.* Sault Ste. Marie, ON: Beth Crane, WeMakeBooks.ca.

McCullough, D. (2013, November 1). *American Christmas Memories - David McCullough and the Mormon Tabernacle Choir.* Salt Lake City: Mormon Tabernacle Choir.

Moore, B. (2009). *Praying God's Word, p. 6.* Nashville, Tennessee: B&H Publishing Group.

Pfeiffer, G. (Director). (2005). *Human Edge, Facing the Dead* [Motion Picture].

Pfeiffer, G. (2005). *Human Edge, Facing the Dead,.*

Seidemann, K. (2004, September). Arno Ambel --Musical Pioneer. *Articulation - The Arts Council of Sault Ste. Marie, p. 3.*

Simpson, A. B. (2010). *HIMSELF: The Glorious Reality of Christ in You.* Celebrate Publishing.

Soviet Deportations from Estonia. (N.D.). Retrieved from http://en.wikipedia.org/wiki/Soviet_deportatio ns_from_Estonia#June_deportation_of_1941

Stories, C. N. (2013, December 8). *Nelson-Mandela-Dies-at-95.* CBN News - Christian Network.

Tallinn. (N.D.). Retrieved from http://en.wikipedia.org/wiki/Tallin: http://en.wikipedia.org/wiki/Tallin

(n.d.). *The Singing Revolution.*

The Singing Revolution (2006). [Motion Picture].

The Singing Revolution (2006). [Motion Picture].

The Singing Revolution (2006). [Motion Picture].

Truman, H. S. (1956). *Memoirs by Harry S. Truman, Volume One: Years of Decisions.* New York: Double Day and Company.

Viirlaid, A. (n.d.). *Graves Without Crosses.*

Viirlaid, A. (n.d.). *Graves Without Crosses, p. 76.*

Waples, R. (1982, April 17). *Starlite.*

Waples, R. (1996, September 9). Sault Opera impresario honored, but no swan song. *The Sault Star.*

Waples, R. (Sept. 13, 1993). Sault Ste. Marie: The Sault Star.

Waples, R. (September 9, 1996). Sault Ste. Marie, ON: Sault Star.

Sault Opera: Zorba 1993 2004.10 Scrapbook 55 Courtesy of Sault Ste. Marie Public Library (ssmpl.ca)

Made in the USA
San Bernardino, CA
27 October 2014